DREAMS

DO

EXIST

THE EDUCATIONAL AUTOBIOGRAPHY
OF DARYL C. SMITH

WRIITEN BY DARYL C. SMITH

D0061718

For more information address Deeandro, LLC, PO Box 1536, Owings Mills, Maryland 21117.

Published by Daryl C. Smith, Randallstown, Maryland

First Edition
Graphic Cover Designed & Page Layout by
Elgin Guthrie, Never Ending Productions, Inc

Photographic Consultant by
La Kaye Mbah, Soulstice City Photography

Editing Consultation by
Maritza Lenard

Library of Congress Cataloging-in-Publication Data –
Processed.

ISBN 978-0-615-21255-5

Dedicated to the memory of My Mother

Ruby Alberta(Smith)Saunders

(Aug 13, 1942 – Sept 21, 1997)

For your support your love

your words of encouragement

And keeping my promise to you

"Daryl's mother - Ruby Alberta (Smith) Saunders (1942-1997)"

Dreams Do Exist

"Daryl's father - William "Chuck" Gross (1943-1971)"

Dreams Do Exist

"Daryl, you shouldn't be afraid to dream because you could awaken one day and find out that it's a reality."

Tommy Dunbar
K.C. Royals
Spring 1990

Table of Contents

Home Plate

Acknowledgements:

I would like to thank the many people that encouraged me to keep my dream of writing this book a reality.

The Family:
My Immediate family: – Rochelle (Ro), my wife, Taylor, my daughter, my sons, Sterling and Daylin.

My sisters: Kareen, Michele & Ruth; My brother: Jim Jim – thank you for sometimes "hiding" the truth so that I could pursue my dreams. I love all of you.

My uncles: Smitty, a true father figure then and now & Peetie often offered words of wisdom. I truly thank you and love you for that…

Special thanks and love for all of the support through the years to: Jimmy, Ellen, Aunt Baby Sis, Aunt Puddin, London, Asia, Joycee, Stevie, Roy ,Butter-roll, Mornie, Teena, Beverly, Sissie, Lady, Tina, Loretta, Aunt Minnie, Aunt Dorothy, Aunt Edna, Vanessa, Stephanie, Tonya, Aunt Ray, Shawn, Little London, Tiesha, Martitez, Porsha, Warren, Little John, Trinity, Lavoy, Lavaughn, Lavelle, Larry, Sherri, Craig, Candace, Cameryn, Ronny, Tony, Thelma, Jimmy, Duane, the "Rev", Donnell, Darrell, Celestine & Tracie.

The Baltimore Crew:
William Hawk, William Long, the late great Elrod Hendricks - who never turned his back on me; Cousin Hank Johnson & Bernard White. Brooks Robinson, Paul Blair, Eddie Murray, Dave Johnson, Joe Klein, Cal Ripken, Jr., Billy Ripken, Scott McGregor, John Stefero, Tippy Martinez, Dennis Martinez, Ken Singleton, Al Bumbry.

Northern High School coach – Late Manny Warner, Mr. Ross, Dr. Brenda Johnson.

Northwood Little League – Mike Meglinson, Valerie Meglinson, Mr. Walker, Marie Owens, Willie Nichols.

Dutch Village Joe, Dennis & Keith Caldwell, Gary, Danny, Tony & Curtis Levere, Big Tony Chestnut, Ms. Loretta, Ms. Levere ,Ms. Louise, Bernadette, Carla, BB Gerald bka Kung Fu, Rodney, Audrey, Phil.

Harford Park Little League – Mr. Phipps – thank you.

Wilson Park Raiders Pony League – Joe & Timothy McFadden, Madeline McQuay, Micheal McQuay, Tony McQuay, Phillis & Deborah McQuay.

Elite Giants - wow what a team- Leon Fields, Lawrence "Money" Monroe, Tim Holley, (currently, Athletic Director Gilman), Mike Lewis, Menvile Rhodes, Craig Holt, Dwayne Fowlkes, Terry Little, Gil Stanton, Cheese, Steve Williams, Curry Cheeks, Bernie Bowers, James & Larry Trent, Dewayne "DJ" Johnson, Dana Barnes, Reynard Brown, Trench Davis, Mo Smith, Alan Howard.

Cozy Corner Baseball Team – Henry Johnson, Sr.

Baltimore Softball Crews
Just Us Softball
Panthers Softball
Renegades Softball

The Florida Crew:
Ms. Floyd, Lisa , Cola ,Tracy, Monique, Damion, Mello, Kirby, Rob, Curt, Little Curt, Lampkin, Mr. West, Ms. Graham,

Harriett, Robin, Mr. Wimbelton, Ron Frier, Mike, Cyrus, Joe, Nip, Peanut, Mr. Lamar, The Down Beat Crew. The MIAMI Softball Crew, Charlie, Phillip, Umpire Ms. May (Lester Hayes Crew). Judge May.

The Baltimore Skins Golf Club

The Daryl Rouse Foundation (Pittsburgh) Golf Crew

Darryl Strawberry Autism Foundation

Fairway Fellas Invitational

Forest Park First Tee Program

Ernest "Fish" Brown Foundation

The Konan Kids Foundation

The Teams & Coaches
I would like to personally thank Linvel "Mo" Moseby, Curry the Yankee Rebels, Coaches Fran & Joe; Hertz All Stars - Frank Slivka and son Joey who followed me to the end. Sherriff Falbo, Coach Billy Hunter and Mike Gottlege at Towson state University - awesome people. Joe Consoli - my scout who always had my best interests in mind.

Special Thanks
Ms. Pam & Ms. Veronica, Elgin Guthrie, for the best graphics ever, Ralph and Brenda Wright, Jackie White Smith, Pastor Sandy Blake Ushery, Dr. Richard Schlesinger and Dr. Jennifer Schlesinger, Shirley (Morgan State Intern), LaKaye Mbah, Kelly Davies, Pat Bayton

Elena and Tommy Schlegel – the greatest fans ever who followed me through my entire career and friends today – thank you!

First Base

Learning the Ropes

I was leaving home for the first time. That meant I would no longer have daily home-cooked meals from mom or grandma. However, the thing I would miss most was the indescribably -delicious dessert, especially the ones prepared on Sundays. About the only thing I could cook was a hard-boiled egg, and I would let that cook until it had a crack in it. A gourmet cook I was not.

The farthest place I had been from home was Kings Dominion in Virginia. Needless to say, I had more than a plane ticket and bonus coming my way. My date to report to training camp was February 15, 1980. The Texas Rangers had already sent my airplane ticket and signing bonus with the guidelines to be followed by all players living at the Holiday Inn in Plant City, Florida. There was also a ticket that said limousine service. Wow I thought - a limousine! Who would have guessed? At nineteen years old, I was beginning a career as a professional athlete. I had never been to the airport before, let alone on an airplane. I had always been fascinated by airplanes, but terrified by them at the same time! Nevertheless, I boarded the 727 Eastern Airline plane headed for Tampa, Florida. I must admit, when the plane started backing up in preparation for its take off, I was shaking in my shoes. Taking off felt like a roller coaster. Just like a roller coaster, we went straight before the big dip came. I held on as tight as I could. I couldn't believe it; the couple next to me was so relaxed. Once we got into the air, I was fine. I was already feeling a little homesick.

When I finally arrived in Tampa, it was sunny and nice. Everything had gone just fine. After picking up my luggage, I went outside to meet my limousine. There I was holding onto my ticket, which said "limousine services." I noticed several other guys who also looked like baseball players. Some of them had duffel bags that said "Rangers" on them. I stood and watched as some of them loaded up in two shuttle vans and pulled off. I was expecting to see a nice limousine waiting for me. Then this older gentleman came over to me and said, "You're a ball player, aren't you?" he asked. "Yes sir." I replied. "Why didn't you catch one of the two shuttle vans?" he asked. Now I'm looking real silly. He then informed me that the second shuttle van that left was the last one for the evening. "That was the limousine?" I asked. "They sure were." he replied. "Don't you have a ticket?" he continued. "Yes, it's right here." I said. I handed him my ticket. "Well you missed it." he informed me. "You'll have to take a cab." He said. "No way." I said. So I took a cab to Plant City, Florida. When I stepped out of the cab, I had $57.00 less in my pocket! Thank God I at least knew the name of the hotel. Since I had enough sense to get a receipt for the cab ride, the Rangers gladly reimbursed me. When I was walking to my assigned room, I passed some of the guys who I had seen in the airport. "We didn't know you were a ball player." a voice from among them stated. "Yes, I am." I replied.

That night, the players, mostly veterans, started to get really noisy right from the start. Questions began flying all around me. "Oh yeah, where are you from?" one asked. "What school did you attend?" another inquired. "What round did you go in?" another voice from the crowd spoke out. "How much did you sign for?" another asked. "What position do you play?" someone wanted to know. Things were moving so fast that all I could think to say was "I'm not really up for talking right now. Look guys, I'm tired. We can talk about this stuff some other time." I said. Boy, talk about being under a microscope!

I finally got to my room, which had double beds in it. No one was in the room. I unpacked my clothes using every hanger and every drawer in the room. I didn't stop to consider what my roommate would use to put away his clothes. Finally situated, I was too tired to go out to grab a bite to eat. Dinner needed to be

quick since I had to get to bed. At 8:00 the next morning, I was due in the clubhouse to get fitted for my uniform. I called for room service. My first night's dinner was nothing to write home about. I guess you could say it was an "All American" meal - it consisted of a burger, some fries and a can of Coke. At last, it was time for bed!

By 11:30 p.m., the lights were out and the chain was on the door. I was just falling asleep when the door opened as far as the chain would allow. "Who is it?" I asked. "Can I help you?" Actually I was scared as heck. I had no idea who was at the door. "Hey, open the door." the voice said. "I'm your roommate." I turned on the lights and let him in. "Sorry," I said. "I didn't think anyone would be coming in this late." "I missed my limousine." he said. "You too?" I asked, half laughing to myself.

His name was Lenville "Mo" Moseby and I'll never forget him because although I had used every hanger and every drawer in the room, he didn't make a big deal about it. It turns out that he remembered what it felt like to be a rookie. And he remembered all the mistakes he made as a rookie. "You're a rookie, aren't you?" he asked. "I guess I am." I replied. Mo said, "Don't worry about moving your stuff until tomorrow. I'm tired. It's time to hit the lights. I'll talk to you in the morning. Get some rest. You'll need it."

After Mo told me to "get some rest because I would need it," I became very curious and couldn't sleep. I waited until Mo got into bed before getting out of bed. I turned on the lights and said "Hey Mo, what did you mean when you said that I'll need my rest?" Mo replied, "Oh that's right, you're a rookie. Well, rookies have it worst because they have a lot to prove." I asked, "What do I have to prove, and to whom?" Mo replied "Daryl, I hope you don't think that this is going to be a piece of cake because unless you're a "bonus baby," it won't be." I knew that a bonus baby was a number one or two draft pick who usually was given lots of money upfront and who got a lot of attention from the coaches and that was definitely not me. "Oh," I replied. I'm a pitcher and I'll throw hard." "Oh, so you have some cheese with you, huh?" Mo asked. "What are you talking about?" I asked. "No, I don't have any cheese with me" I retorted. "I was talking about baseball." Mo said. "That's what I'm talking about also, I replied. When you're a pitcher and you throw hard, we call your pitching cheese or gas. "Shooter, please remember that, because if you don't, when the other guys get finished teasing you, you'll have tears in your eyes." Mo replied. "Shooter, one more thing, don't let some of these brothers talk crap to you about anything." Mo offered. "They will try to intimidate you just to see if you can handle it." He continued. "All right Mo, thanks for the tip." I replied.

Mo stood about 6'4"and two hundred and forty pounds. He was a huge brother from Pecos, Texas. It was his third year in the minor leagues. I felt like I was half his size at 6'4" and two hundred and twenty pounds. After trying to pick Mo's brains for all that I could before my first day, I found out that Mo was a third round draft pick out of high school. So we did have at least a few things in common. We were both African-American, both pitchers, and both of us were drafted right out of high school. By now it was 2 o'clock in the morning, and I was still trying to find out what to expect the next day and the whole summer after that as a matter of fact! My next question was answered with a loud snore. I guess I wore him out with too many rookie questions.

Day One of Training Camp
I didn't own an alarm clock, but Mo did. At 7:00 a.m., it went off. Mo said, "Shooter, you take your shower first and wake me when you're finished. "Okay I'll do that." I said. After I finished showering, Mo went in. By the time Mo was finished showering,

Dreams Do Exist

I was dressed and had already made my bed. Mo asked, "Who made your bed, the maid?" "No, I did." I said. Mo just laughed and said "Shooter, you better stick close to me today." "Why?" I asked." Mo said, "You might get lost going to breakfast. And by the way Shooter," he continued, "we do have maids that come by everyday to clean the rooms, which includes making that bed of yours! Let's go eat."

Breakfast and dinner were provided by the team in the Holiday Inn's restaurant every day. Breakfast was from 6:45 to 7:30 a.m. Shuttle vans then ran from the hotel to the park, every fifteen minutes. There was no reason to miss breakfast or a ride to the park. Everyone had the same thing for breakfast, lunch and dinner unless you chose to eat somewhere else, which was hard to do unless you lived on your own during spring training. You also had to sign your name whenever you ate at the hotel. There was always a coach or manager sitting at the hotel door. They would rotate who was posted at the door so that everyone in team management would get to see and know the players. I was certain that they also paid attention to your table manners and your personal appearance. If anyone was skipping breakfast or dinner, he would be confronted about it and he better have a very good reason why.

After breakfast, it was pretty hectic while getting uniforms because it must have been over one hundred and twenty guys in line. There were four lines, one line for each of the four ball clubs – Rookie Ball, A-Ball, AA-ball and AAA-Ball. All the pitchers and catchers were together in the bullpen and all the outfielders and infielders on other fields. I would say that there were about sixty pitchers all bidding for a spot on each team, with each team only carrying a maximum of eleven pitchers.

All pitchers stretched together. There were seven pitching mounds in the bullpen and four pitching coaches there. All of the coaches were checking out the pitchers to see what kind of velocity and control they had on their fastballs. Fastballs, that's all we threw for the first four days. We threw for about ten to twelve minutes for the first two days with a day off from throwing on the third day. The third day was filled with pitching drills.

During this time I was feeling anxious because to me the sound of the ball popping into the veteran catcher's mitt was a sound that appeared to be much greater than the sound that my fastball made. Throwing resumed on the fourth and fifth days for about fifteen to twenty minutes each day. At that point, I could see why they asked us to report to camp in shape. I was in the first group of pitchers and I think all of us were rookies because we were assigned high numbers like seventy-six, sixty-five, and sixty-seven. One guy even had number eighty-six. No, I wasn't the guy who had eighty-six. For my height and weight, I had a pretty good fastball. Considering the fact that I was a rookie, my eighty-two mile per hour fastball had pretty good control. The only thing that caught my pitching coaches' eyes was my delivery. The head coach said my pitching was wild and funky! In other words, I was all leg kick. The pitching coach's name was Richard Such. He was also known as "Suchie." I never called him Suchie because Mo told me that only the white guys called him that. Mo felt that the guys, who called him Suchie, were doing so because they wanted to get on his good side. I decided that my play would speak for itself. I didn't need to try to get on the coach's good side!

Laying the Foundation

If there's one thing that stuck in the back of my mind it was something that Money, my coach from the Elite Giants told me. He said, never kiss anyone's butt. You may have to squeeze it a little bit, but never kiss it!

I was surprised when Such came over to me and said "Young man, slow everything down. You're moving too fast and you're all out of sync." I replied, "Such, this is the way that I've pitched all my life." Such laughed and said, "If you keep on throwing the ball like that, you'll never become a pitcher. There's a difference, you know." "Yes sir," I replied. "And another thing son," Such said, "don't call me sir and I won't call you son."

Afterwards, I finally slowed down my funky motion while also no-ticing that some of the older pitchers were laughing at me. It was now time to be a spectator and watch the other pitchers do their thing. Mo was up next because he was in the "A-Ball Group." The first pitch that Mo threw popped the catcher's glove so loud that it spun everyone's head around and everyone started watching him throw. His balls were popping eighty-eight to ninety miles per hour easily, and his delivery was so slow and smooth. The first thing that I thought was how lucky I was to have a roommate who knew the system and how to pitch. After the "A-Ball Group finished, two of the pitching coaches took all the rookies and A-ball guys on another diamond to practice pitcher's fundamen-tals. I was in the middle of the pack of about twenty-two pitch-ers. The first two rounds of comeback ground balls went very smoothly. By the time the third and fourth rounds of balls started coming back, they were a little bit harder. Guys were getting hit on the shin and other places. I seemed to think that it was funny, because I was a good fielding pitcher. Until I had a rocket of a hopper hit back at me. The ball hit me right in the groin. Down I went like someone chopped down a tree! The trainer hustled out to the mound and sat me up on my bottom. He wrapped one of his arms under one of mine and his other arm across my chest and picked me up just enough to drop me back to the ground. He repeated the action again! I was in some kind of pain. Once I felt better, I went over and got a drink of water. It was then time for lunch. I had a sandwich, some soup and a couple pieces of fruit.

One day while the pitchers were working on covering first base, I messed up and dropped the ball. I started laughing. My pitching coach didn't think that it was too funny, and that's just what he said. "Smith, do you think this is a joke?" "No." I replied. On my very next turn, I did it again. Only this time I tried to flip the ball with my glove instead of the correct way. I must have struck a nerve or something, because the coach threw down the bat and pulled me to the side. He told me "If you think this is funny, I'll have your black butt on a plane back to Baltimore so fast, it will make your head spin!" I couldn't believe what he said to me.

After lunch, it was time to catch baseballs in the outfield. This wasn't much fun at all because you had twenty-two pitchers and about three of them were hitting balls to the infielders with Fungo bats. The rest of us were chasing down the balls that hit off the bat of the positional players. As far as I was concerned the only things that resulted from this activity were suntans and tired legs! After batting practice was over, all the pitchers would change into their running shoes to end the day being observed by the pitching coaches. We usually had a running program. Some days we would run for distance or sprints. Some days we would run foul pole to foul pole for at least twenty laps. Other days the pitching coach would give everyone a ball and we would all line up in a single file and take off running behind him. Coach Such loved doing that type of running. He would stop just between right and right center field. Each pitcher would toss him their ball one at a time and sprint fast forward as if you were a wide-receiver going out for a pass and catch the ball in your glove. We did that about twelve to fourteen times each.

By the end of the day, all you would want to do is lay down and rest until dinner was served. During dinnertime, most of the guys would just sit around and talk about what kind of day they had at the ballpark; those that had a good day anyway. The rest would either go to the game room and shoot pool or play Pac-Mac or some other type of video game.

Everyone who stayed at the hotel had a curfew. The lights and television had to be off at midnight. Most coaches and managers didn't mind if you watched television past midnight, just as long as you were in your room. That night after dinner, Mo and I were sitting out by the swimming pool talking about any and everything concerning life, particularly life in the Minor leagues. We must have talked for four hours. By the time we finished, it was around 11:30 p.m. on a Wednesday night. Four players drove up by the pool. One guy said, "Hey Mo, it's ladies night, do you want to hang out with us?" Mo said, "It's only the first day of camp. You guys are going out already? No, thanks. Have a good one. Later!" Mo yelled. "You see Shooter that's the kind of crap that doesn't get you anywhere." Mo confided. I knew at that minute that I was very fortunate to have someone like Mo to show me the ropes and not lead me in the wrong direction.

We talked about the consequences of getting caught breaking curfew. Mo said that he knew of, and had heard about guys who had to paid fines of up to one hundred dollars for breaking curfew. There were also guys who paid their fines by running the next day until they dropped. In some cases, guys were released from the team for not following the rules. Some guys would go out to a bar and end up getting into a fight. Guys were known to show up the next day at the ballpark with a black eye or a busted lip. Some guys even showed up with stitches.

Spring training was nearing an end. There was one week left until the end of spring training. After that, the teams would be pretty much set. Both Mo and I had been having a good spring. "Well Shooter, Mo said, the next few days aren't going to be too happy around here for some people." "What do you mean, Mo?" I asked. "Tomorrow's cut day and some people are going to be sent home. Don't leave your stuff at the yard. Some people will steal it if they are cut from the team. Bring your good stuff back to the hotel with you," Mo urged.

The Early Days – Asheville

The next morning while the van was pulling up to the field, several coaches and managers were standing outside the clubhouse with notepads in their hands. I asked Mo what was going on. "Don't worry, Mo said. You'll be okay. Just keep walking."

I couldn't help noticing that a guy started to cry after receiving a pink slip of paper from a coach. That's when everything that Mo had cautioned me about clicked in. For that guy the whole spring training had suddenly become a waste and his career was instantly over. Dreams gone and shattered. He probably dreaded going home to face his family and friends. He was probably contemplating working a regular nine to five job. Mo used to say that the Minor League beats working a nine to five job any day! Some of the new guys in their first year didn't make the team. Fortunately, I did, and so did Mo.

All teams were set and the names were set. The names of the players were posted on the bulletin board. I was moved up from rookie ball and placed in A-ball. Mo was upset because he didn't make the Tulsa, Oklahoma AA-ball club. Instead, he and I were going to Asheville, North Carolina to pitch on the same ball club. I felt sad for Mo because it would be his third time in four years going back to A-ball. It didn't seem to matter that he pitched great against some AAA ball clubs. They said he had some control problems and that if he got it together, he would be moved up before the year was out. "They always say that crap," Mo stated.

That night Mo said, "Shooter, I'm going out." He asked me to be his cover. I said, "Sure." Mo showed me a trick that another player named Bobby used to do all the time. He took the extra two blankets that were in the room and rolled them up like a body and placed them under the covers of a made-bed. He also placed a stocking cap over the end of a pillow to make it look like someone was just asleep. Boy did Mo teach me some tricks of the trade!

I must say it worked very well because it even fooled me! At one point during the night while watching television, I turned over to talk to the body in the next bed. "Mo, are you watching television?" I asked. I forgot that I was really alone. That was one night I will never forget!

We arrived in Asheville, North Carolina. The ball club put the players up in a hotel and gave us three days to find an apartment. If you didn't find an apartment in three days, you had to start paying for the hotel room yourself. Sometimes it would take some guys five or six days to find an apartment. When this happened, they would move into a teammate's hotel room and split the cost of the room.

Mo had connections. During the first day in Asheville, Mo took me to meet some older women who lived near the ballpark. These women rented out rooms in their homes to baseball players. I'll never forget their names or the street. The street was Madison Avenue. The names of the four women were: Mrs. Harris, Mrs. Ray, Mrs. White and Mrs. Margaret. They were four of the sweetest and kindest old women that you could ever meet. Rent was only one hundred per month, and you could actually jog or walk to the ballpark.

There were only nine African-American players on the team that season. Some of the players wanted more privacy than a rented-room would provide. Other players didn't want to stay with these women because they would not allow players to have women in their rooms unless they were married. Mo stayed with Mrs. Ray. Dirty Reds stayed with Mrs. White, and Bobby Ball stayed with Mrs. Margaret. I stayed with Mrs. Harris. Mo and I moved out of the hotel the next day. The other players looked for apartments for many days. The apartments everyone eventually found were basically in the same neighborhood.

After I moved in and got situated, I called my mother to give her my new address and phone number. I told my mother everything before she could ask. I told her how exciting my first year of spring training was. I also shared how I learned a new pitching form. My mom and I had only spoken to each other about three of four times during the spring. I never told her about the run-in with the pitching coach and his comment about sending me home. She would have lost it had she known. She would have found out who he was and seriously given him a piece of her mind! We spoke of Mo and how he helped me through the whole spring with nothing but sound advice. I also told mom that I skipped rookie ball and went straight to A-ball as a reliever.

Mom said, "That's wonderful sweetheart, but may I ask you some questions now?" "Sure," I said. "What in the world is A-ball," she asked. I thought you were going out for the Texas Rangers." I laughed because mom didn't know anything about the Minor Leagues. The only two names she knew were the Texas Ranger and the Baltimore Orioles. I had to explain to her about all the different classifications of baseball before you get to the Major Leagues. Mom was flabbergasted. She said that all of that stuff, the different levels, sounded too complicated to her. "So tell me about Asheville," mom asked. "Well, it's nothing like the Baltimore city, but the people I live with and the neighborhood remind me of home" I answered. During my first season in Asheville, my manager was Mr. Terwillerger. He was the third base coach for the

Minnesota Twins. Mr. Terwillerger was a very emotional manager. He would only argue at the obvious bad calls. When he did argue, the whole park would know that something went wrong!

My first year was basically a learning stage. I was ahead of some and others were ahead of me. It also reminded me of spring training where pitchers would often face hitters who were several years older. However, the sooner you were able to overlook someone's age, the better off you were. During the games, I would watch every starter while he prepared for the game. Every pitcher had a different style and pattern of warming up. Some guys would stretch for fifteen to twenty minutes, depending on the weather. There were other guys who could just pick up the ball and go at it! Those guys usually didn't make it through the season without injury, because they never stretched.

All teams stretched before batting practice every day. If there wasn't batting practice that day, you would still stretch as a team. Managers would usually leave it up to the team to pick a team leader for stretching. Others would just rotate the leadership responsibility. I think that I was very fortunate to be able to play with so many guys in my first year that had already played college baseball.

You could only imagine what a team of rookies look liked trying to get something accomplished. The sight was amusing even though in some cases; you had college rookies who had just been drafted with great talent. Division A games usually lasted for about three hours because of the number of runs scored and the lack of quality pitching. Some pitchers worked fast and others were quite slow. In the Minors, you are taught to pitch at a steady pace so that your infielders don't get too complacent.

Asheville had a short right field fence. It was about three hundred feet. Managers would try to stack their pitching staff with left-handed batters. After my first year, I learned how to pitch to lefties in that park very quickly. Our ballpark wasn't the best field in the Sally League, but it wasn't the worst either. Whenever we played at the very nice stadiums, we seemed to shine a bit more. Maybe it was the bright lights or the nice green grass. It also could have been the fact that the stands were packed, whenever we played the Yankees in Greensboro, North Carolina. Just about every town we visited was nice. More important than the town, however, was the hotel where players practically lived for three months. It got real boring pretty quickly when we didn't have a game. Most towns had nice malls and sport shops because players would always need something. I don't know how many times that one of us forgot something important like a jock strap or a cup, and would have to buy another one from a local store.

On the weekends, most malls would be closed after a game, but the movie section would stay open. Some guys would go to the movies after the game. A few guys would find more ignorant things to do. For instance, I remember going to the mall to catch a movie with one of my teammates. We arrived about thirty minutes before the show started. We decided to window shop to kill some time. Shops were already closed and their gates were down. Ten minutes before the show was supposed to start, my teammate told me to go ahead to the movie, he would catch up to me. I did just that. When he finally made it to the movie, he had a white bag with him. I asked him what he brought when all the stores were closed. I never got an answer. But I decided not to go anywhere with him ever again!

As a professional baseball player, dealing with fans could sometimes be challenging. Most fans don't mean any harm, but some do. I was once told that no matter what a fan says or does that it shouldn't bother you unless contact is made.

My favorite fan didn't get on my case but did get on Tommy Dunbar's case every time that we played the Greenville Braves. He would tease Tommy every chance he got. When Tommy would attempt to bunt, he would shout from the top of his at least eighty-one year old lungs "That's it Dunbar, you just showed everyone that you can't hit!" If Tommy would strike out, he would count Tommy's every step back to the dugout. When Tommy was in the batter's box, he would say "Hey Tommy, have you ever stolen a watermelon?" Not only would the fans laugh, even the manager would laugh. That same fan would travel about three hours to Asheville, to our games. If his home team, the Braves were playing us in Asheville, he truly became everyone's favorite fan. During the last home stand of the season against the Braves, he brought at least ten watermelons to the hotel where we were staying for some of the players, and definitely for Tommy. For some players, those watermelons got to be pretty expensive. They would spit their seeds off of the balcony and onto the cars in the hotel parking lot. Because most summer days were about 95 degrees, the seeds stuck to the paint on the cars. Consequently, the resulting fine would have to be enough for two paint jobs. The first job would be to remove the seeds; the second job would be to apply a fresh coat of paint.

One perk of being in the Minor League is that you get to meet so many different people from different places. For instance, we often traveled to the West Coast. There were more Mexican players on the West Coast teams as well as players from Colombia and Venezuela. It was really great because I've even had managers from Canada and Puerto Rico. I've even had managers it seemed who were from Mars, but that's another story! As you could imagine, the ability to speak and understand Spanish would have been really helpful.

One of the unpleasant things you have to deal with in the minors is team fights. In some case the fights caused people to get hurt. I've been involved in good ones and bad ones and even a few really unpleasant ones. Fights would start for a variety of reasons. If a batter hit a home run and didn't start running until he finished admiring the ball sail over the center field fence, there was a real good chance that he would be knocked on his butt the next time he faced the pitcher. His teammates would even be prepared for the retaliation and would do whatever it took to protect one of their own.

An example of a bad fight happened during my first year. I was involved in the second worst fight that I'd ever seen in my twelve minor league seasons. The fight was against the Mets in Shelby, North Carolina. There were zero outs in the top of the seventh inning with a man on third base. The count was 0-2 on the batter, who by the way had already been hit once that night. The pitch was high and tight. The batter went down and the ball went all the way to the backstop! While the batter was on the dirt, the runner and the pitcher were racing for home plate. The batter got up quickly and charged the pitcher who was coming in to cover home. Boom, the batter caught the pitcher with a right forearm shiver under the chin! The pitcher was knocked out cold. Too bad he never got a chance to cover home! The batter thought the pitcher was charging home plate to get him. Both benches cleared and we fought for at least forty minutes off and on. Both teams were fortunate enough to have enough players to finish the game.

Around the neighborhood, another player and I were busy trying to learn how to cook and learn how to use Mrs. Harris' gas stove. I remember one night; two of us were trying to turn on the stove to bake some TV dinners. Mrs. Harris told us to move out of the way and let her show us how to turn on the oven. Not knowing that the gas had been on for about five minutes or so, Mrs. Harris struck a match and attempted to light the pilot. The next thing we heard was a loud boom! The oven lit up like a fireball and caught half of Mrs. Harris' hair. The stove was lit, but we feared that she was hurt badly. She assured us that she was okay and encouraged us to finish baking. Mrs. Harris went upstairs while our TV dinners were baking. Fifteen minutes later, she returned downstairs with her head fully wrapped in white gauze. My buddy saw her first and started laughing hysterically! I turned around and said, "Oh my Lord, Mrs. Harris, maybe we should take you to the hospital!" I could not laugh at her because she looked like she was in pain. One of my teammates who owned a car took her to the hospital. Thank God she was not seriously hurt.

The women on Madison Avenue were the sweetest women in the world! They sure made it easy for the players on the Asheville Tourist. Most of our salaries started at eight hundred to nine hundred dollars per month. The Madison Avenue ladies were kind enough to only charge us one hundred dollars per month for rent! That really helped us out. We would talk to our friends in the AA Division, and they would tell us that rent in Tulsa, Oklahoma was anywhere from four hundred to six hundred dollars per month! Playing in Asheville, North Carolina definitely represented the good old days! Typically, the higher your baseball salary, the higher your rent.

Second Base

Spring Training 1982

By now I had gotten my feet wet with my first season out of the way. Despite having a terrible year, I knew that both the Rangers and I were pretty sure that I had learned something. My skills had improved greatly, particularly my pitching. I remember the first day of spring. All of my pitching coaches were congratulating me on how much I had improved my mechanics. I was grateful that they noticed!

During the spring, I lost plenty of friends either by trades or guys just being released. Unfortunately, Mo happened to be one of those friends. Words could not express the way I felt for him. After all, Mo was my first roommate in the Minor Leagues. He always showed great concern for me, while offering excellent and honest advice. I'll never forget what Mo said before he left that day. He said "Shooter, it's been real." He advised me to never underestimate anyone. "Peace." that was his final word to me as he headed out the door.

As camp ended and the teams announced who was going where, I ended up going back as expected to Asheville, North Carolina for the start of my third season. I was full of confidence as the third season got underway. I remembered that Mo said if you win ten games, more than likely you'll be promoted.

When I arrived in Asheville, I contacted Mrs. Ray, the woman whom Mo had stayed with. I didn't contact Mrs. Harris who I had stayed with my first year because she didn't allow you to have women visit you unless you were married. After all, Mrs. Ray wasn't as tight on the guys who had stayed with her in the past.

I was primarily used as a reliever for the first month and a half. By the middle of May, so many guys were getting hurt or moved to the Major Leagues, that I was placed in the starting rotation. I had a record of one win and two loses but my ERA was at 1.76. Our record as a whole wasn't that great either. It was more than simply a good time to take advantage of the starting spot. It was also a great opportunity to take advantage of the deal that Mrs. Ray had offered me. For every game that I won, Mrs. Ray would cook me a breakfast that I wouldn't forget! I don't know how much Mrs. Ray's offer had to do with it, but I went on to win ten games in a row! Naturally, I became ace of the staff. The free breakfasts from Mrs. Ray not only gave me some added weight that I truly needed, they also happened to include some very unexpected encounters. Mrs. Ray would sometimes miss sitting the breakfast tray evenly on my lap, which would cause the orange juice to spill. But how could I complain, it was free food, and it was the thought that counted to me. She didn't have to do it at all! My eggs and toast didn't taste that bad soaked in orange juice.

Mrs. Ray and I had this very special bond. I remember when I used to pay my rent to Mrs. Ray. A disease had left her partially blind in both eyes. I would fold the ten-dollar bills once, the twenties twice, the fifties three times, and the hundred dollar bills were left unfolded. Taking this extra effort to assist her in counting her money was no trouble at all. I was always amazed at how Mrs. Ray could find her way around and about so easily. I would see her at the grocery store and baseball games. By this time I had acquired my own little fan club at the ballpark. My fan club consisted of the homeowners from Madison Avenue.

By July I was really feeling like I had been in one place for too long. So many things had changed during the course of the season. We had five African-American pitchers on the team and all of us were in the starting rotation. That's something that you may never hear of again and definitely something that you will never see at any level especially at the Major League level. When we played other teams, guys would tease us and say that they hoped the lights were good because all of the African-Americans were dark-skinned except Dirty Red. He was high yellow.

On my birthday I received a birthday cake shaped like a baseball, and I received all sorts of goodies from my fan club of Madison Avenue. All of my teammates were dying to get a piece of the cake even though it had an African-American pitcher on it. I didn't play on my birthday, and I was in such a hurry to talk to my Mom that I grabbed my cake and hurried home. I totally forgot that the guys wanted some of the cake. When I phoned home, my sisters were all there but said that Mom was out. They wished me happy birthday, and ended the call.

The next day I carried the cake back to the park untouched. That day I had a run in with my back-up catcher while batting practice was going on. The back-up catcher was Carmello Aquao. He was a short catcher and utility infielder from San Juan Puerto Rico. It just so happened that he claimed that I was hitting his infield ground balls too hard to him. I reminded him that this was the same way they hit during the game. My manager agreed with me. I guess that seemed like a challenge to Carmello. He told me to hit the balls even harder! I accepted the offer and the first ball I hit hopped up and hit his lip. Carmello went running into the locker room looking for the trainer. I had no time to go over to try to help him. Everyone was laughing.

When I got to the locker room, Carmello was on his way out. I asked, "Carmello, are you okay?" He did not reply. He just walked straight for the bat rack and grabbed a P-72 bat. I ran towards the mountains that surrounded the field. Everyone was still laughing. They thought it was funny to see a 6'2" guy running from a 5'5" midget. However, anybody with good sense wouldn't stand in front of a crazy, hot-tempered Puerto-Rican!

It only took one glance directly into Carmello's eyes to realize that he was dead serious. For some reason when you are scared, you usually run a lot faster. I made it to the top of the mountain in left field so fast that you wouldn't have believed it. I stood at the top of the mountain trying to catch my breath. Carmello was yelling up at me. I heard him say that he was going to take a crap in my new glove. I didn't think that he would do something that absurd.

Batting practice ended and I was tired of standing on the mountain. I finally got up enough nerve to come down. I knew Carmello was crazy and that I would have to watch my back. My manager, Mr. Robinson, pulled Carmello and I into his office and told us to cut the crap. He went on to inform us that if anything else happened from that point on that we would have to answer to him. That would definitely mean double trouble because Mr. Robinson was a big guy. In addition to physical punishment, we could also be required to pay a hundred-dollar fine. Mr. Robinson was overly concerned about all of his players. That's something that's hard to come by in the Minor League!

During the game, I had this weird feeling to call home. I asked my manager if I could use the phone for a brief moment to check on my mother. I had not spoken with her in three weeks, which was unusual. Mr. Robinson gave me permission to use the phone. When I dialed the number, no one answered. Before I left the locker room, I told Mr. Robinson that no one was home.

Suddenly it dawned on me what Carmello said while I was on top of the mountain. I checked my locker to see if he was bluffing. You wouldn't believe what that little midget did in my brand new glove! I was so shocked that someone could be so nasty to do something like that! I politely went back to the dugout.

The game was about to end and there were only two things on my mind. I needed to call home again. I also needed to pay Carmello back for what he did to me! I don't think that anyone else would have been as patient as I was. When I returned to the locker room, the guys were preparing to take their showers. I acted as if I did not know what Carmello had done. I had everyone fooled. The guys were dying to see my reaction when I found my glove.

I waited until Carmello made his move towards the showers. Just as he was coming from the other side of the lockers, I met him in front of the showers. I smacked him right on top of the head with the glove! I guess I just lost it. Carmello charged me into the showers. I beat the crap out of him while he was naked.

Mr. Robinson heard the commotion and came into the locker room. He had us both by the back of the neck as he explained how he would not tolerate this behavior in his ball club. We were both fined one hundred fifty dollars for the fight. I was the last one out of Mr. Robinson's office. By the time I finished showering, Carmello had already left. When I got back to my locker, there were still a few guys hanging around. While I was talking to the guys and getting dressed, my pitching coach came over to the locker and asked for a piece of the birthday cake. As I pulled the cake down from the top of my locker and sat it on the bench, my coach and I noticed that there was a hole right in the center of the cake. The plastic that covered the cake was also pulled back. I had no idea where the hole came from. Finally, one of the guys told the pitching coach not to eat the cake because Carmello had tampered with the cake before he left the locker room. I tossed the cake into the trash and went to talk with my manager about the day's events. My manager lifted my fine and doubled Carmello's the next day! That officially ended my friendship with Carmello. I also wouldn't allow him to be my catcher when I pitched. I phoned home to speak with my Mom. As my sister answered the phone and said "Hi," I also heard her say, "Its Daryl, what should I tell him?" I said, "What's going on? Where is Mom?" Finally my oldest sister Karreen got on the phone and informed me that mom had a heart attack and she was in isolation at Greater Baltimore Medical Center. My mom was 18 when I was born and felt that her parents and her older brothers could take care of me more than she could. My father was in the Army and was away from home often so he couldn't take care of me either. Although my mother and father never married they lived in the same community and I often bounced from one grandparents home to the other.

The funny thing is it really didn't bother me that much since I was supported and loved by two sets of grandparents and aunts and uncles on both sides too. Kareen told me not to worry about Mom and that they would take care of things at home. She wanted me to continue having the great year that I was having. At that time my record was thirteen wins with three loses with a 2:21 earned run average (ERA). I had also been listed as one of the pitchers for the All-Star Game which was being played in Macon, Georgia. I was scheduled to pitch in two days at home in Asheville.

As I waited for our next game, I got very little sleep. My eyes were blood-shot red and I was very weak. As game day approached, there wasn't any change in my mother's condition. I had not spoken with anyone on the team about my mother's condition, not even my manager, Mr. Robinson. On game day I showed up at the park earlier than I was supposed to. We were taking batting practice and Mr. Robinson was throwing the ball.

I walked into the locker room and packed my bags taking everything out of my locker. Then I walked across the field in the middle of batting practice. As I neared the right field line, guys on the opposing team asked me what I was doing. I guess they thought it had something to do with the problem that Carmello and I had. Someone in the crowd yelled "You sissy, where are you going?" I said nothing. By now Mr. Robinson had run over to the right field line and stopped me in my tracks. He asked, "What's wrong? What are you doing?" Tears were rolling down my face like rain.

As I stuttered with pain in my speech, I simply couldn't get the words out. Mr. Robinson walked me into the general manager's office and shut the door. I gradually told him of my mother's heart attack. He sympathized with me and said, "Would you like to call home?" I told him no one was home. I explained that I wanted to catch the bus home to see my mom. I was only making nine hundred dollars a month in my third year so a plane ticket was out of the question. In addition to my small paycheck, I had too many bills and had paid too many fines.

Mr. Robinson called my sisters who shared the news with him about my mom's condition. As he wrote down a number and hung up, he dialed another number and handed the phone to me. The voice was weak but familiar. I said "mom, are you okay?" "Yes, I'm fine son, just a little tired," she said. "I'm going to be just fine," she continued. My Mom was a very heavy smoker and she also had high blood pressure. This is a disease not only known in my family, but one also known to many African-American families. As the conversation ended, my tears and pain eased. Mom said, "Sweetheart, just do what you have to do there, and the Lord will take care of things where I am." At that moment, I knew that she would be just fine!

Mr. Robinson took the phone and wished my Mom a speedy recovery. After he hung up the phone, he said "Your Mom said to remember the three C's." Mr. Robinson didn't know what she meant, and he didn't ask. She meant "calm, cool and collected". The next day after I pitched a complete five-hit shutout, I read that Mr. Robinson told a reporter that he was impressed with my performance, especially after all that I had gone through in a week's span. Mr. Robinson concluded the interview by saying that "I was calm, cool and collected out there tonight." The article brought a smile to my face that I will never forget. That game was my fourteenth win with only three losses during the 1982 season.

As the season continued and the dog days of summer set in, I started looking for a promotion to the AA League in Tulsa, Oklahoma. The promotion would get me out of the bus leagues of A-Ball. The South Atlantic Salley League had some of the worst bus rides in A-Ball. Most of the time the buses that were rented had no air conditioning. These older buses often broke down on long trips.

For the first two or three hours on the bus, traveling without any air conditioning was not a problem. However, if we had to travel ten hours to Macon Georgia on one of these busses, the bus would almost certainly break down! Once the bus got fixed or a new bus arrived, it was often past midnight. Since more often than not we would be in the middle of nowhere, our only option for food would be a truck stop where the food was anything but fresh!

I don't know what was scarier, getting off the bus at the local truck stop or eating stale sandwiches. We would stop so that more than one guy could use the rest room at a time. We would also have a chance to grab a quick bite to eat. Twenty minutes was the time limit to get back on the bus or you would risk being left. Many guys often missed the bus!

1982 was all but happy anyway because of all the killings going on in Atlanta, Georgia. During that time I remember asking the guys on the team to wear a piece of green ribbon on their jerseys in memory of the killings that were happening. Half of the professional sports teams and others were doing the same thing. Some guys complied and some guys didn't.

I remember August of 1982 the most. That's when I had my second run in with my pitching coach. The Texas Rangers released Mo. I was so ticked off because I was losing a good friend. I told old man Raybourn that the team was prejudice against African-Americans. I told Raybourn that African-Americans would never go anywhere in the organization. I guess it didn't take long before Raybourn told my pitching coach what I said. My pitching coach confronted me about my comments against the team. My mouth just dropped to the ground. The coach then went on to say "you're right. And since you feel that way, I'm going to make sure that you get sent back to A-Ball until you rot, no matter how many games you win." Not feeling intimidated I asked, "Are you done?" I walked away from him. That night we did not say one word to each other.

On my next start, I was trying to win my sixteenth game. With three weeks left in the season, I still was not promoted. We were in Spartanburg, North Carolina playing the Phillies A-Ball Club. I had a no hitter pitching into the seventh inning when I heard this voice while in the middle of my delivery. The voice said "hey Daryl Smith, the man from Atlanta is looking for you nigger." I couldn't believe my ears. The voice was so loud that it caught the attention of several players that were in the dugout at the time.

They popped out of the dugout to see who would say such a rotten thing. At that moment, I knew that my ears were not deceiving me. I glanced at my left shoulder to see if my piece of green ribbon was still pinned to my jersey. It was. I looked into the stands only to see some idiot waving a green handkerchief at the field while leaving his seat. Some of the guys were yelling at him. However, he just left the stadium. I never found out who that guy was or where he went. All I know is that anyone who could be so cruel probably didn't have a heart anyway! The next batter shattered my no hitter. However, I managed to get my sixteenth win of the 1982 season. I was ahead of another pitcher, Baron James, who pitched for the Yankees. He had fifteen wins. There were still three weeks left in the season. I tied the league's record for sixteen wins in a season.

At the end of the season, I still had only sixteen wins. I lost two out of the last three games with one game called a no decision. Each game was a heart breaker because I was winning each of them but left the game with men on base. I couldn't complain because my bullpen had not let me down all season. The most heart breaking loss of the season came after pitching almost nine innings of my last game. With the score five to three and men on first and second, a reliever gave up a first pitch home run to the number nine hitter. That lost was a tough break! The other pitcher, Baron James ended up tied with me as well, but he had sixteen wins and six loses. I don't recall what his ERA was. Nevertheless, we turned in two of the best pitching seasons in a long time in the Salley League. I still ended up with the league's best record that year at sixteen wins and five losses with a 2.76 ERA.

Saying goodbye to teammates at the end of the season was a hard thing to do because for a hundred and forty games, sometimes more, you've eaten, showered and protected each other through thick and thin. You become attached to your teammates. After all, you spend more time with the players than with your family. Most families weren't allowed to travel with the teams in most organizations. It's real tough on families in the Minor Leagues because at anytime you could be called up to AA or AAA ball. If you were called up, you would have to break your apartment lease and pack up and move. Some guys would have to drive their families to a new town. In some cases, players would have to report the very next day to their promotion spot because a player was hurt and they had to play the next day. In that case the player would leave his wife and family to pack up and meet him at his next destination. That was a tough scenario.

After the season was over, it was good to head home. It was really good if another player was going to the same town or in the same direction and one of you had a car. The team usually paid for your airfare home. If you knew someone who had a car, you could use the airfare to buy gas for the car ride home, and pocket the savings. Some players would use the savings to treat themselves to a good meal. By the end of the season most of us were sick of fast food and looking forward to a home-cooked meal!

I knew that I was returning next season. I was also told that I would be one of the pitchers attending the winter instructional baseball camp. Instructional ball was pretty boring. However, the experience was invaluable because you got a chance to play against top quality players.

After I got home, the three-week break went by so fast! I learned that I was to receive an award sponsored by TOPPS in Sports Banquet. The award was called Maryland's Star of the Future Award. It was a great honor. Many professional baseball players from Maryland had already received this award. Moose Hass, Harold Baines, Cal Ripken Jr., Billy Ripken, Milt Thompson and a host of others were past recipients of this award.

Things were going fine once I arrived at instructional camp. I was pitching great. I saw great batters like Daryl Strawberry and Tim Rains every week. There were a lot of Major League players there. Some were doing rehabilitation; others were there to work on one skill or another. The Expos and the Rangers shared the same clubhouse that year. It was partitioned off for each team. Every now and then, the major league skipper would come by to see the players in the Minor Leagues and their games. At the time, the skipper happened to be Don Zimmer. Zimmer fell in love with a pitcher named Ron Darling.

Darling was a number one draft choice out of Yale. It seemed as though Darling grabbed Zimmer's attention every time he pitched. Whenever Darling was pitching, Zimmer would be there. After Darling finished pitching, I would get a chance to show my stuff. Unfortunately, Zimmer never got to see what I offered as he always left immediately after Darling finished pitching.

Towards the end of instructional camp, I met some new people. Tim Rains was one of those people. He was working on base stealing while also helping his Expo teammates. Tim advised me to never give up on the dream of getting into the Major Leagues. He said that even after I told him about the incident I had with my pitching coach. It was the last two weeks of instructional camp and the Hanshin Tigers, from Japan came into town to play against the American players. It was great to get a look at the Japanese players because they did just about everything different from the American players. They would do so many exercises before the game. For instance, the players would warm up for ninety minutes by jumping and hopping around before batting practice. Then after that was over, they would take batting practice and all of the players would run until it was also game time.

I'm glad I had the opportunity to start two of the games that we played against them. In the first game I pitched five innings and didn't allow a hit or a run. In the second game I only allowed one run on three hits in five innings. It was great because the Japanese players were disciplined and scrappy hitters. They always tried to execute in each situation.

There were about four games left against the Tigers when one of the Japanese coaches approached me and said, "Great pitching the other day." He said, "Your name is Smith?" I laughed because I didn't think that he could say it any better than that. I said, "Yes, that's my name. What's your name, I asked?" "Tom Fuekura," he replied. "Nice to meet you." Tom then went on to ask, "Would you like a Hanshin Tiger hat?" "Sure." I replied.
"Would you like a hat from our team?" I continued. "Yes," Tom replied, "I would." I ran to the clubhouse and asked the trainer for a new hat. When I returned with the hat, Tom was holding a sheet with my statistics circled. "This is you, yes?" he asked. I answered, "yes". "You had a great season." Tom commented. "Thank you." I replied. "Would you like to play in Japan next season?" Tom asked. My mouth just fell open. "Are you serious?" I asked Tom. "Yes," he replied. "we would love to have you. You would make a lot of money with us." he continued. I asked "How much are you talking about?" "Sixty thousand to sign and one hundred twenty five thousand for one year," Tom replied. My heart skipped three beats because in 1982 the Major Leagues salary wasn't even close to that amount! A Major League player was only making sixty two thousand five hundred a year. The signing bonus he was offering was almost that much alone! I said "That sounds great, but I don't know if the Rangers would let me go after having such a good season." Tom said, "You don't need their permission to quit. That's all you have to do." I told him that I would give him an answer the next day.

That afternoon I went right to Tim Raines and told him about the offer from Tom. Tim and I talked for about twenty minutes while sitting in the outfield. Tim told me that if I quit playing in the U.S. that I would be ineligible to play in the U.S. for three years. "What if they sent you back after your first year?" he asked. "You would then be out of baseball for two years." He reminded me. Tim knew what he was talking about. I knew that I had a lot to consider before making a decision. Tim also mentioned that since I just had a great season there was always the possibility of playing in the Major Leagues.

I thanked Tim for his advice and later that night I called my mom and my uncle. They both agreed with Tim that I should stay for my own well being. My mom mentioned the fact that it was only my second year away from home and if I did go to Japan, I would more than likely experience culture shock. The next day I declined Tom's offer and vowed to stay in the U.S. This is the first time that I've publicly talked about the offer. During the off-season I waited each day for a call from the Rangers or my farm director, Joe Klein. I never received the call I expected. I was not placed on the forty-man roster or invited to Major League camp.

It was two weeks before the Topps in Sports banquet where I would receive my award. I called Eddie Childs, the owner of the Texas Rangers to remind him of the banquet and asked if he planned to attend. He said he planned on attending. However, no one from the Rangers organization showed up to see me receive my award. My family and I were very hurt. We didn't even receive a phone call. I expected more from the Rangers.

After the winter meetings, I received a phone call from Joe Klein, telling me about my next year's assignment. Klein was not only my Farm Director, he was also a Baltimorean. It's funny because I never heard of him until after I signed with the Rangers. I've always trusted Joe because he wouldn't talk to you in circles. Joe would tell you just how it was. "Joe, when am I going to move up?" I asked him. "You're not," he replied. "Why, Joe?" I asked. "You need a third pitch," he continued. "I have a third pitch and a fourth too," I responded. "Yes, but you must perfect those pitches or else you'll go nowhere in the game," he replied. I knew he was telling the truth!

During the winter I had to work even though I was still staying with my mom. I've always worked to help out no matter what. I've worked different jobs just about every winter. I worked in a pool hall one year. I worked in Rite Aid for three years. Working at Rite Aid was a good experience! I would get my job back each winter and was also promoted when I was with Rite Aid. The job was only three blocks from my house. I even worked at a big security firm for about seven years.

As a security officer, I was allowed to carry a shotgun and hand-cuffs. No one in baseball knew what type of work I did in the off-season. For more than two years I even worked as a store detective at Montgomery Ward. It was fun but hard work at the same time. As spring approached, I finally received my assignment for the following year directly from Joe Klein.

First promotion to AA Ball

At the start of the 1983 season, I was playing as a starter in Tulsa Oklahoma. I remember having the off-season privilege of working out with the Baltimore Orioles. It was after I received the Maryland Star of the Future Award that I was introduced to plenty of people, many of them professional athletes. Both Brooks Robinson and Elrod Hendricks attended the award ceremony. After the award ceremony, I had dinner with Robinson to discuss the possibility of me signing with the Brooks and Ron Shapiro Agency. They were agents for most of the Orioles and Pirates. I signed with them after our meeting.

At the start of spring training, I had a guaranteed starting position coming. After two weeks of camp, I came up with tendonitis in my right shoulder. This was the first injury of my Minor Leagues' career. After visiting the doctor's office, I was told to rest for at least two weeks. I was sent to Florida to rehab my arm.

For two weeks I rested from throwing. I did all types of arm exercises, and instead of feeling left out, I felt better toward the end of camp. The AA Tulsa ball club had already broke camp while I was still in Florida. Because of my injury, when I resumed playing, I was the first started. The weather wasn't too bad, just a little cold. We played Darryl Strawberry and the Mets. They had a good team and at the time we had a record of zero wins with four losses. They beat us pretty good that day! When the Mets left town, all five starters and three relievers had ERA's above 6.00.

I was the youngest pitcher on the staff that year and Tom Burgess was my manager. Tom wasn't a soft manager by far. He would always say that a young fella like me should always feel good. However, as a matter of fact, my arm was killing me and I neglected to tell anyone. That wasn't smart on my part because it could have ended my baseball career! Some managers act as though young guys should never get hurt.

There were so many disappointments my first year of AA ball. Our team played poorly and we got our butts beat just about every night. Additionally, AA teams stopped flying their players to games and started having us travel by bus. Some rides would seem to take forever, especially when we had to travel for eighteen hours to play in El Paso, Texas. It didn't matter that there were fold-up beds on the bus. Most guys would show up one hour before the trip just to get a bed. If you ask me, none of us deserved a comfortable ride with an eight and forty-two record!

At that time my record was two wins and five loses with a six something ERA. Other pitchers had higher ERA's. I remember once just before we were to take an eighteen-hour trip to El Paso, several of us decided that the bus trip would be too long. The night before we were supposed to leave, we got together and sabotaged the bus. It was funny because the guys who did it were the last ones to show up at the park for the trip. When they showed up, there were big smiles on their faces. Two hours later we were on a plane to El Paso for a five game series. Man those were the days! Even though El Paso has one of the most difficult ballparks to play at in America, we won four out of five games. The bus however was waiting for us after game five! I lost the last game in El Paso. I was then demoted to class A baseball in Burlington, Iowa. Talking about breakdowns, I broke down in tears! There were guys who had lost more games than I had, and who had worse ERA's!

I asked my manager why I was demoted. My manager could only say that it was because I was the youngest. Give me a break! The whole pitching staff stunk! Our hitters would score eight runs and the pitchers would easily give up ten runs. This was my first demotion. Later I would find out that it was all part of the system called "the numbers game." So many players, good and bad ones, got caught up in the numbers system. If an injured player is sent down to AA ball, a healthy player would be put on the disabled list for as long as it took the injured player to get through rehab. That's life in the Minor Leagues!

My flight to Burlington, Iowa was one of the worst I ever had! I wish I had taken the bus. The intensity of the landing felt three times worst than a normal landing! I was petrified. Burlington wasn't much to speak of except for the fact that the players in Burlington had a winning attitude and a better approach towards the game than we did. That attitude helped me get myself refocused and back on track. I flirted with a couple of no hitters and went on to finish the season with six wins and two losses with an exceptional ERA.

After many changes that year at the AA level, the 1982 Tulsa Drillers drilled their way into first place during the second half of the season and ended up winning the Texas League Championship. Even though I spent two and a half months of the season with them, it had no effect on what happened during the second half of the season. I did not receive a ring! Some guys were only with the team for two to three weeks and they received a championship ring! It didn't seem fair. I had to believe better days were ahead. But before those days would come, I had a rugged off-season training program.

All during the off-season I worked and worked and worked! After the season, I received my old job back at Rite Aid. After being back for just one month, I received a promotion. It was great, but I knew that I would be leaving again in six months. It was a very cold winter, but pitching in the Baltimore Orioles tunnel seemed to warm me up a bit. I even had the opportunity to work out with guys like Jim Palmer, Dennis Martinez, Scott McGregor, and Tippy Martinez. Elrod Hendricks helped me out even though I wasn't an Oriole. The experience was great!

Spring Training 1983

I had a normal spring. There were about sixty-five guys fighting for forty jobs on the pitching staff that year. After having a good spring, I expected to go back to Tulsa AA to prove myself with some serious authority. Over the past three years I gained twenty-five pounds and was slim and trim with better pitches and mechanics. Nevertheless, I was optioned out to the San Diego Padres in Salem, Virginia. I said to myself, "Not A-ball again!" Sometimes you just have to make the best of the situation you are dealt! Most of the older guys would say that as long as you were wearing a uniform, you still had a chance.

The Carolina League was full of talent and trouble! The Padres had eighteen players from their organization and the Rangers had six. Most players on that team from the Rangers felt like misfits. It was strange to always play in front of coaches and managers who had nothing to do with our organization. It's a sour feeling

when teams combine organizations and you share everything as if you are one organization. It's called a co-op. It wasn't too bad for me because I just took advantage of the fact that other ball clubs would get a chance to see me. I remember starting against Dwight "the Doc" Gooden at home in Salem and at his home park, which was Lynchburg, Virginia. The Doc operated on the whole team with nineteen strikeouts. I walked with the score still zero to zero in the eighth inning. I tried a little humor since nothing else seemed to be working. I said "guys it's almost time to take the bus back to Salem, who wants to go? We're leaving right now. Forget this game, I continued." Everyone started laughing. I guess it loosened them up because we ended up winning the game one to zero. Before that every player had his mouth wide open in disbelief.

The Major League Mets and Padres were playing at Shea Stadium and the Mets organization flew both my team and the Lynchburg Mets to Shea to play in a pregame. It was great! I had a chance to meet and talk to a lot of talented guys full of inspiring words. I spoke with Darryl Strawberry who I had known and played against in the Texas League. Sometimes when I think about it, I was moving backwards while I was honestly trying to move forward. There was nothing that I could do about it at the time. So after the Doc did his thing to our team again by striking out players, I had dinner with my teammates. We flew back the next morning and played again that night.

Two months into the season management from the Rangers organization started showing up to evaluate their players. They also wanted to test them for drug use. That meant trouble for some guys. Sam McDowell, a former pitcher was working with the Rangers to help players get a grip on their lives. Sam was the only player to be kicked out of baseball because of alcohol use. Sam taught guys how to visualize. It was an experience that I'll never forget! We had private sessions which started by staring at dots in a circle while trying to picture ourselves completing games or hitting a home run in a very tight situation. Anything that would make you oblivious to what was happening around you. Sam also picked out the guys who were using drugs. He said that you could tell if your buddy was drinking too much alcohol by pinching him on the arm or leg. If you pinched him and a bruise appeared for more than a few days, he was probably drinking too much. Well I wasn't about to go around pinching anybody! By now I was tired of seeing the San Diego World Famous Chicken and Sam's act too. Sam's only success was in making already tense players even more tense! Everyone knew that he was there to eliminate the weakest among us. However, thanks to the visualization tips, my concentration and velocity increased greatly. My fastball was between eighty-eight and ninety two miles per hour, with average control. That alone earned me a promotion back to AA ball in Tulsa, Oklahoma half way through the season.

My return to the league in Tulsa went well. My farm director, Joe Klein, who was also Vice President of Baseball Operations, greeted me upon my return. It was a perfect return because I pitched eight strong innings and received the win. For the next month and a half, I was watched by over ten different scouts and important people in management throughout the organization. There was talk of me possibly doing some relief in the Major Leagues. Wow, what a change! I now had a chance to make a big jump. There were two months left until the end of the season and things were still looking good. My fastball was still popping. I had great snap on my curveball, and good control of my changeup.

In a game against the Shreveport Giants, a power hitter named Rob Deer touched every starter on the team for a home run or two except me! In the seventh inning I became a victim of a line drive by Deer and that almost ended my career. I was taken to the hospital after not only being struck near the elbow, but also falling on the same arm while trying to brace my fall. The doctors put a splint cast on my right forearm to help the circulation. The doctors also mentioned that the ball just missed shattering my elbow by a fraction of an inch. I thought, boy what a break!

After leaving the hospital with my manager and trainer, I learned that I was more than likely going to be promoted to the Major Leagues before the year ended. The next morning as I tried to lift my toothbrush up towards my mouth to brush my teeth, I couldn't even lift the toothbrush above my chin. I had so much pain in my right shoulder that I dropped the toothbrush. I tried once again but I still couldn't brush my teeth. The pain was real.

For the last month of the season, I stuck around instead of going home. During that time I learned some exercises to help my arm regain its strength. The exercises were those of a well-known doctor named Dr. Jobe. Rehabilitation consisted of different types of exercises using dumbbells and rubber stretch tubes, which I used for the rest of the season and during off-season. I couldn't work at the start of the off-season because I had not regained strength in my arm and I was attending physical therapy.

A friend had recommended Richard Schlesinger, the Orioles' team doctor to me. I went to him for a second opinion. The team doctor for Rangers wanted to cut in and file down the bone on my shoulder that was causing me to have an impingement. Dr. Schlesinger said that he could avoid having to do surgery. Like any pitcher or player would be, I was extremely happy! As we took the strength test, I was informed that my left arm was at least sixty percent stronger than my right arm. The results called for a Cybex machine which I would get use to using four times a week. I was also being injected with Zilocane, which was supposed to help speed up the process. This wasn't the type of off- season that I had in mind. However, as a professional baseball player, you have to accept the good and the bad that comes. After two months of treatment, I felt so strong. I felt like I could pitch nine innings. Dr. Schlesinger mentioned that there would be days when I would feel bad because of the amount of strength that I had to regain. The Rangers and I stayed in touch during the off-season and they were also being sent information on my progress, which was good news.

By the fourth month of my rehabilitation, I was really feeling great. I regained all but fifteen percent of my normal strength and was able to use my arm in a pitching motion on the Cybex machine. I had never met such a wonderful group of therapists in my life! They put so much confidence and ambition into their patients and their job. I was soon able to begin my post-season practice to prepare for spring training. I was cleared to begin throwing but at a slower pace than normal.

I was fortunate to be able to work out with the Baltimore Orioles as they too were preparing for spring training. I was also fortunate to be under the watchful eye of the Orioles bullpen coach and ex-catcher Elrod Hendricks, who watched over me with a very special eye even though he had others to watch in his organization. I was well known by most of the Orioles ballplayers, Ken Singleton, Eddie Murray, Mike Flannigan, Tippy Martinez, Storm Davis, and John Stefero, who worked out at Memorial Stadium during the winter. Three weeks into my post-season practice, I was up to fifteen minutes of throwing off of the mound. I was still timid about cutting loose the fastball and snapping the curve ball even though my arm felt fine.

Then with one week left before the Orioles were to leave for Florida, Elrod had me wait until everyone else was done to throw on the side while he served as my catcher. Before he put his gear on he said, "The only way that you are going to find out what you're afraid of is to let it go." With Elrod as the catcher, I began to practice throwing fastballs. I let it go and it felt great. I'll never forget Elrod for giving me lots of attention and for helping to re-store my confidence! He changed my approach towards my style of pitching.

As the Orioles went south, I continued to prepare for Minor League camp. It was still kind of cool in Baltimore as I began working out with the Towson State Tigers Baseball Club. Their coach was Bill Hunter. Once again, I must admit that I was very fortunate to get an opportunity to work out with another program. As I continued to work out, I remembered that Dr. Schlesinger told me to keep up the exercise until I regained total strength. However, I never actually felt like I regained one hun-dred percent of my strength. In the two weeks of training with Towson State, I felt great. I didn't have any problems striking out anyone and my control was good. At the time, I felt as though my velocity was consistent with how I was now pitching after the injury.

Third Base

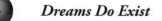

Third Base

Spring 1984

I said my goodbyes to all my family and friends as I headed for spring training. The only thing that I could really think about was how I would do. The first week flew by. All my teammates and the coaching staff were pleased with my hard work and accomplishments during the off-season. Spring training was going well. For most of spring training, I felt great until I started losing strength in the last week of spring. I was put on the radar gun one day and my top velocity was seventy-two miles per hour, sixteen miles per hour off of my speed before the injury. It was interesting that my arm was not hurting at all. I couldn't understand it. I called Dr. Schlesinger and explained to him what was happening. Dr. Schlesinger told me "just keep up with my exercises and stretching and you should be alright."

The Rangers were pretty fair with me through all that had happened to me while I was with them. Even though Joe Klein had left the organization, I was pretty well known by the new staff, including the new Farm Director, Tom Grieves. Tom was a sweet-spot hitter from the late 1970's to the early 1980's. A sweet-spot hitter is one who gets hot and cold very frequently. I was told that Tom would do very well in June, then in July he would get shut down.

After being set back in my fourth year of spring training, I lost my spot with the AA club. Shifting players between the Minor Leagues and the Major Leagues was happening pretty regularly. Typically, if a Major League player became injured, the spot would be filled with someone from the Minor Leagues.

After spring training, I was forced to take another job in A-ball. It was a choice that was very hard to make because I was tired of A-ball and really didn't feel as though I had anything else to prove at that level. All I really needed was a good and healthy season in AA ball which seemed harder to come by in 1984.

I moved to Burlington, Iowa. After spending the first two months of the season pitching really well, I was promoted back to AA ball in Tulsa Oklahoma to try and help out their team. After eleven innings and eleven runs, I was demoted back to A-ball in Burlington Iowa. Now it was really getting harder to take. A friend said to me, "Don't worry, as long as you have on a uniform, you have a chance." The thought registered in my mind. Yeah, he's right, I thought. Anything could comfort me at that time.

As I returned to A-ball, I started thinking about my pitch selection and what was and wasn't working for me. My mechanics and rhythm were fundamentally sound. All I needed to do was ban my worst pitch and start concentrating on the rest. That's exactly what I did! I banned my curve ball that had brought me thus far in my career and started working on my fourth best pitch, which was my forkball. That decision turned out to be very fortunate for me not only in 1984, but later in my career. I flirted with two or three no hitters the remainder of the '84 season.

After deciding to make the forkball my number two pitch, I finished the season in A+ ball with a six and two record and a very decent ERA of two point sixty-two. During the season, management would ask if there was anyone interested in winter ball. I signed up hoping that I could get a chance to go and work on my forkball and make some easy money. The pay was about $3,500/month with no tax deductions. Winter ball was also recommended by one of the staff members who wanted to see me blossom the following year.

On November 3rd, I received a call from Colombia's winter baseball team, Cartagena, asking if I could be ready to play in two weeks. "Sure." I responded. I flew to Colombia right away and was given two weeks to prepare for my first start.

It was my first time out of the country and I was nervous and excited at the same time. As I remember, the flight was very long and my journey from the airport to the hotel was scary and even longer than the flight. I was happy that I had taken several flu shots before I left Baltimore. I heard of rumors of people getting sick once they left the United States. During my trip to the hotel, I passed a small town about every thirty to forty miles, and it seemed as though everyone was awake. There were lights everywhere as though it was the middle of the day. Loud music was playing and people were moving around as if it was 10 o'clock in the morning. I couldn't believe it.

When I arrived at Hotel El Conquistador, the only people I saw were the police. I asked the cab driver "Why are there so many police in this town?" He simply stated, "Tourist." As I checked into my hotel room, I was placed with two other baseball players named Ricky Coleman and Tom Dozier. Tom was leaving in the morning. It was his spot that I was taking on the roster. Each team had seven Americans. Six of the seven players on the team would later play in the Major Leagues. Cecil Fielder, Bill Pecotta, Dave Johnson, and Tom Dozier were among the players who would go on to play in the Majors. Cecil wouldn't play until the team assured him that they had sent plane tickets for his wife and son to join him in Colombia. Cecil was having a great winter with the team. The talent on the team was great and each game was packed with fans.

I was pitching well. I was gaining great control of my forkball and had started throwing a split-finger fastball. I remember making a road trip just before the playoffs. We stopped on the way back to Cartagena to get something to eat since most of us were starving. The American players would usually wait until we got back to Cartagena to eat, but not the Hispanic players. They would eat everything the pit stop had to offer.

One night when we were returning from a road trip we stopped for one of the players to grab something to eat. He ran in the back of a little building that also sold sandwiches. Everyone on the bus was asleep except for the manager and me. As I watched him, he returned with this fairly large package that was the size of a turkey. As he passed by me, I asked him "What's in the bag?" He replied, "You don't want to know." So we left it at that until he fell asleep and my curiosity got the best of me. I climbed on top of the seat so that I could reach the overhead section where he had placed the bag. I stuck my head in the bag. I began quietly peeling open his bag trying to remove the tape from the package just right so that I could put it back the same way that it was. As I pulled the last piece of tape from the package, I lost my footing and the package hit the floor with a loud thump. The bus driver turned on the lights and there on the middle of the floor laid a whole cow's head. I screamed at the top of my lungs! Everyone on the bus woke up at this point. As first there was a stunned silence. Then they started laughing because they knew that I had stuck my nose into someone else's business. The owner of the package simply said "I told you that you didn't want to know, didn't I?"

I had never seen so much poverty in my life as I saw in Cartagena. It was a crying shame and it really made me realize how fortunate I was to live in the USA. I also saw my very first bull fight. It was fun to see but very sad at the same time. The following day after the bullfight, there was this crazy event. I witnessed twenty men trying to remove a sack of money from on top of a bull's head. So many people got hurt trying to get that sack!

One week before the start of the playoffs, while we were taking batting practice, I noticed a very dark, low cloud coming directly towards home plate. It sounded like a large truck was approaching. Ricky Coleman was standing next to me and I heard him say the word "bees." I'm not very fond of bees because as a child I was stung very badly by several at once, sending me to the hospital. I took off running for the dugout. My manager, Jose Martinez started running towards me yelling. "Get down. Get down! Everybody lay down on the ground." I noticed the sound was getting louder. Everybody was lying on the ground watching me run for the dugout. I decided to hit the deck and pray that the loud sound would go away. Thank God it did! The bees landed on the right center field fence. As everyone entered the dugout, our manager informed us that they were killer African bees. If you got stung, you would more than likely die!

The fire department set the bees on fire. It was the only way to get rid of them without harming anyone else. Once the firemen were finished, we resumed the game. Yes, winter ball my first year was an experience!

Off Season 1985

After returning home in January, I was laid off from pitching for one month to take a break from the wear and tear that pitchers so often put on themselves. I hit the gym and continued my running and my rehabilitation. Towson State University had begun workouts as they always did early in the fall. Thank goodness they did because the Orioles had changed some faces in the front office. I was not allowed to workout with Elrod Hendrix and the rest of the Orioles pitching staff. Management informed me that I wasn't part of the organization. So instead of getting some special attention from Elrod, I headed out to Towson State every day, even if I wasn't pitching batting practice that day.

I felt as though it was time to try and turn over a new leaf. I had a new woman and a new attitude. I was working full-time as an inspector for a black-owned security firm, Howard Security, where my girlfriend worked as well. I worked out very hard every day because deep in my heart I knew that I could make my dream come true. Howard Security knew that I had played baseball for six seasons. They had no idea, however that I was planning on returning to baseball. That was always a big problem with getting a job just for the off-season. You always had to be a little creative and hope for the best. Most companies wanted to know about your past jobs. Sometimes they also wanted to know about your future plans.

I earned two promotions within three months, moving up first to Chief Inspector and then to Field Supervisor. My girlfriend knew that I would be leaving soon for spring training. It was now February and I had already signed a contract to play AAA ball for the 1986 season. I had begun throwing at Towson State three times a week. As it neared time for me to report to Minor League camp, I turned in my two weeks notice. Howard Security, the company in which I was employed respected my decision to pursue my dream to become a major league baseball player. My girlfriend was acting as if she didn't care that I was leaving. It was kind of bothering me that no one said much to me on my last day. As I clocked out, someone called me to the back office. Most of the crew was gathered in the back office all bunched up just to wish me good luck! It was very thoughtful of everyone to gather to wish me well. I spent the last week before camp packing and saying good-bye to family and friends.

Spring Training 1986 Arizona

My first day in spring training I learned that my god-brother, Stewart McCoy had been drafted by the Chicago Bulls, and was expecting a child by his girlfriend of three years. It was great news because we had been very close since my junior year of high school. However, all of the good news couldn't relieve the heat from the Arizona sun! It was very hot. It was also my first time not going to Florida for spring training. The Arizona air was very dry. The mornings weren't too hot, but by the time we started the games it would be cooking outside. After a long day in the heat, the guys on the team were still willing to hang out at night.

This was my first time being in another organization's spring training. I wasn't about to make a bad impression by missing curfew. My new attitude paid off when it came time for me to perform on the field. However, despite having another good spring training at the AAA level, I was still demoted back to AA ball after the Major League made their cuts. I tried to talk to my ex-manager and pitching coach, Jack Aker, but he was too busy in his new role as our Major League Pitching Coach. I never heard anything else from him. Sometimes it seemed like you didn't even exist! You're looked upon as just a number.

As the teams became set, it was time to sign a new AA contract for the season. I waited for my turn to speak with the farm director. I was in line behind my teammate from last year, Doug Jones. I listened as he argued about his AAA contract with the director. He was explaining that he couldn't support his family on the salary they wanted to give him. I don't know if Doug got what he wanted that day, but later that year Doug made it to the Major Leagues! Since then, he has become one of the best five or six relief pitchers in the Majors. The following year he led the Majors in saves. I'm sure that he didn't have any problem taking care of his family after that! After Doug finished, it was my turn to negotiate.

I didn't have a family, but I sure could use more than fifteen hundred dollars a month! This was my first spring training with the Indians. I didn't want to be too demanding. Even though I asked for two thousand a month, I only received eighteen hundred. I couldn't argue with a raise of three hundred dollars! The worst part was that I was going back to the AA level for the third time. Sometimes it seemed like right when things were going well, something would impede my progress. This time it wasn't because of the numbers game, it was because of an injury.

My new role this season was a spot starter and relief pitcher. It was a different year at the same level. We did have a few new faces. Most of my teammates the year before had been promoted or released. Rico Petricelli was my new manager and my pitching coach was a real rough guy named Rick Peterson. My only concern was about our new catcher. I wasn't sure if he could handle my forkball and split-finger fastball. Andy Alanson, my catcher in 1985, was the best catcher that I ever had thus far in the Minor League. Little did I know that my problem wouldn't be my catcher, but my pitching coach, Rick Peterson. I didn't know what his problem was, but we just never seemed to see eye to eye on anything!

As a Pitcher you know what you have to do to stay in shape and yet you still follow the program to make everyone else happy. After all, you wouldn't be hurting anybody but yourself if you cheated. One day, I noticed my catcher looking over at Rick after each pitch. If I would shake off whatever he put down, he would be less likely to put it down again. After quite a few disagreements between the catcher and me, Rick strutted out to the mound. I guess he called himself laying me out, but it didn't stop me from telling him not to call my game. I also had to remind him that I wasn't a rookie. Later that week when I was doing my side work, Rick just sat and watched. He said nothing the whole time I was working out. He just stared at me and I couldn't figure out why. When I finished working out, I started my running program and still Rick had not moved from his spot.

I ran my normal twenty-five minutes that day and as I was heading towards the locker room to change shirts, Rick said to me "Smitty, I think you owe me an apology." "For what?" I said. He said, "You tell me." I replied, "I don't know what you are talking about." Rick went on to say that he could make my life miserable and that I should remember what I said about him to someone on the team. I laughed and walked away thinking of how I was advised never to kiss anyone's butt. Evidently, not everyone on the team was taught that same lesson. I remember telling someone that I thought Rick was arrogant because of the way he walked. It's funny because I wasn't the only one who thought that. Even players on other teams thought so.

As the season went on, Rick and I still weren't communicating. I was pitching well and he didn't bother me at all. One day in Albany, New York, a good three weeks later, everything changed. I was doing my running and Rick called me just as I was in the middle of my stride. I didn't answer and kept running. Before I knew it Rick was beside me grabbing my arm. He asked "Didn't you hear me call you?" I pulled my arm away. I said "I heard you, so what." The center field gate was open and Rick invited me outside the gate to settle our dispute. As we stood on the outside of the left-center field fence, Rick invited me to take a punch at him by pushing me firmly two times. As I zeroed in on his nose, something told me to just walk away. Rick has no idea how close he came to getting his nose broken! I knew I had too much class to fight another grown man. So I did what my conscience told me to do, and I walked away.

During the next home stand, I went out after the game to get some wings and a beer. Granted it was after curfew hours. I thought because we were at home it would not matter that I was breaking curfew. Besides, I was about to starve. Unfortunately, Rick was out on the same late night run. We didn't speak as we gazed at each other. I asked for my order to go. The next day I was fined fifty dollars for breaking curfew. That's fine; I expected that and paid with no problem. It turned out that the wings were more expensive than I thought they would be. Rick called himself getting even, but we didn't have any more run-ins.

My season had gone pretty good despite the issues with Rick. I finished up with six wins and three losses, with an earned-run average of 3.23, on a fifth place team. It was nothing like the team we had in 1985. There were talks of the team not returning to Waterbury, Connecticut for the next season. I'm not sure if the city really wanted baseball there because they didn't fight too hard to keep their team in place. No one from the AA team was called up that year. Several guys were placed on the forty-man roster for the 1987 season.

I waited for my girlfriend to arrive from Baltimore. She had taken a two-week vacation so that we could take our time driving back from Connecticut. I started asking myself if this was all worth it. I was tired of baseball because it never seemed fair when it came to the person with the best statistics or skills to be called up. The game itself was fair, but the promotional process was questionable!

When I returned home after the end of the season, I was more than happy to see my family. I had only seen my family one summer during the seven years of my professional career. As you can expect, my family was happy to see me as well! However, they could tell by the look on my face that I wasn't exactly happy. I was anxious because I hadn't fulfilled my dream to make it to the Major Leagues yet. My girlfriend was happy that I was home! She had seen me here and there during the season. I had gifts for my family from towns that I visited throughout the year. I noticed that one of my sisters was not among us. My three sisters and little brother would always be present for my homecomings.

I ran my normal twenty-five minutes that day and as I was heading towards the locker room to change shirts, Rick said to me "Smitty, I think you owe me an apology." "For what?" I said. He said, "You tell me." I replied, "I don't know what you are talking about." Rick went on to say that he could make my life miserable and that I should remember what I said about him to someone on the team. I laughed and walked away thinking of how I was advised never to kiss anyone's butt. Evidently, not everyone on the team was taught that same lesson. I remember telling someone that I thought Rick was arrogant because of the way he walked. It's funny because I wasn't the only one who thought that. Even players on other teams thought so.

As the season went on, Rick and I still weren't communicating. I was pitching well and he didn't bother me at all. One day in Albany, New York, a good three weeks later, everything changed. I was doing my running and Rick called me just as I was in the middle of my stride. I didn't answer and kept running. Before I knew it Rick was beside me grabbing my arm. He asked "Didn't you hear me call you?" I pulled my arm away. I said "I heard you, so what." The center field gate was open and Rick invited me outside the gate to settle our dispute. As we stood on the outside of the left-center field fence, Rick invited me to take a punch at him by pushing me firmly two times. As I zeroed in on his nose, something told me to just walk away. Rick has no idea how close he came to getting his nose broken! I knew I had too much class to fight another grown man. So I did what my conscience told me to do, and I walked away.

During the next home stand, I went out after the game to get some wings and a beer. Granted it was after curfew hours. I thought because we were at home it would not matter that I was breaking curfew. Besides, I was about to starve. Unfortunately, Rick was out on the same late night run. We didn't speak as we gazed at each other. I asked for my order to go. The next day I was fined fifty dollars for breaking curfew. That's fine; I expected that and paid with no problem. It turned out that the wings were more expensive than I thought they would be. Rick called himself getting even, but we didn't have any more run-ins.

My season had gone pretty good despite the issues with Rick. I finished up with six wins and three losses, with an earned-run average of 3.23, on a fifth place team. It was nothing like the team we had in 1985. There were talks of the team not returning to Waterbury, Connecticut for the next season. I'm not sure if the city really wanted baseball there because they didn't fight too hard to keep their team in place. No one from the AA team was called up that year. Several guys were placed on the forty-man roster for the 1987 season.

I waited for my girlfriend to arrive from Baltimore. She had taken a two-week vacation so that we could take our time driving back from Connecticut. I started asking myself if this was all worth it. I was tired of baseball because it never seemed fair when it came to the person with the best statistics or skills to be called up. The game itself was fair, but the promotional process was questionable!

When I returned home after the end of the season, I was more than happy to see my family. I had only seen my family one summer during the seven years of my professional career. As you can expect, my family was happy to see me as well! However, they could tell by the look on my face that I wasn't exactly happy. I was anxious because I hadn't fulfilled my dream to make it to the Major Leagues yet. My girlfriend was happy that I was home! She had seen me here and there during the season. I had gifts for my family from towns that I visited throughout the year. I noticed that one of my sisters was not among us. My three sisters and little brother would always be present for my homecomings.

I said "This is for Ruth, by the way, where is she?" Everyone got quiet as if something was wrong. It was then that I learned that Ruth had been admitted into a drug treatment program. I felt as though I had lost her for life. After completing the program, Ruth went on to become the manager of a drug recovery house. She remarried and raised three kids. Ruth has been clean now for twenty-two years. I'm so proud of her!

Off-Season 1986

After completing my second year in Waterbury, Connecticut with the Cleveland Indians organization, I returned to work in Maryland. I became a security guard for Montgomery Wards in Towson, Maryland. It was a pretty good job and it paid the bills. I was sharing an apartment at the time, so my bills weren't very high. The hardest part about the off-season was trying not to get hurt. Retrieving stolen property isn't exactly as easy as people think, at times. After security saw a person concealing an item without purchasing it, we would have to view the person leaving the store. Then came the fun part! I would show the person my badge and ask him or her to come back into the store with me. Most of the time it would result in a fistfight, wrestling match or racing competition. The running helped me get in my off-season training. After I apprehended the person, I would bring him or her in our security office and ask for the stolen merchandise. The police then would be called to do the rest of the work. We would always have to show the police the videotape of the theft and save the tape for court purposes. Sometimes we were not able to videotape the theft because it happened too fast. It was a lot of fun working the cameras in the store. I learned quick and started teaching others how to work the cameras. Even though the employees knew that we had cameras, they still tried to steal from the store.

Spring Training – 1987 - Arizona

I prepared especially hard for this season because I was getting tired of being overlooked! This would be my second spring training in Tucson, Arizona with the Indians. I was on the AAA roster for the entire spring and it was clear to see that all of my hard work during the off season was paying off. I was very effective pitching against my opponents. However, as the Major League roster was being trimmed down for the start of the season, I was demoted to AA team that was moving from Waterbury, Connecticut to Williamsport, Pennsylvania. I was told that I would be a starter this year, but for some unfair reason, after a few roster moves, I found myself being placed on the disabled list. Although I wasn't hurt, I wasn't even allowed to practice in the bullpen for the entire month of April. No one in management offered an explanation!

In May, I was taken off the disabled list and given the ball to start. I pitched and as expected, I did not do well at all! I pitched terribly. I expressed my anger in the dugout after I was taken out of the game by throwing and kicking everything I saw. Several players told me to chill out. Other players simply got out of my way! I'm sure that they already knew that I was about to lose it because I had not been pitching, and when I did get the chance to pitch, it was at a very unfair time.

My manager sent a player into the locker room to tell me not to leave the stadium until he talked with me. I left the stadium anyway so that I could get a start on packing my bags for home. This was the first time I had made up my mind to retire from this game. I removed my personal things from my locker. That night my manager came to my apartment with my release papers. I happily signed them and we never discussed anything else about the matter.

I left Williamsport and called the Phillies organization to see if they were interested in me. I had always pitched very well against them and the manager thought highly of me. I was told to stop in Reading, Pennsylvania. This stop was on my way home anyway. The next day I pitched on the side of the Reading Phillies' ball club. After they used the radar gun to clock my fast ball, I was offered a contract and a pay raise from what I was making with the Indians. As I sat in the manager's office, we talked about my velocity of eighty nine to ninety miles per hour and about the role I would play. We also talked about what went wrong with my relationship with the Indians. My manager was also my pitching coach and he helped me substantially. Before I knew it, I was six and zero with a 2.31 ERA, and I was promoted to the AAA League.

At old Orchard Beach, Maine, I learned that a great part of my success came through patience within and from others. That was my first time ever playing at that level. With only one month left, I would get in four starts. My velocity was even higher at the AAA Level. I had one win with three losses that final month. I learned what it took to be a competitor. After the season was over, I was considered a free agent and was immediately picked up by the Chicago White Sox. It sure felt great knowing that I was scouted by another team and had been given very high ratings.

Off-Season 1987

I had a change of heart and decided to try something new and less stressful. I became a used car salesman for Johnny's Used Cars in Baltimore. Of course he remembered me from my teenage years as a pitcher against his summer league team. It was a lot of fun and I was successful selling cars. I sold at least ten cars a week and Johnny allowed me to go to Towson State and work out with the baseball team. I would work out four times a week. After workouts, I would shower and return in a suit and tie ready to sell cars!

My days were long. I worked from nine in the morning until ten at night. However, it was worth it, especially considering that I got to do all of my workouts.

Spring Training 1988 – Chicago

Spring training with the Chicago White Sox was held in Sarasota, Florida. It was a lot of fun that year. We worked extremely hard, and I personally felt great. We did many physical agility tests after practice. All we wanted to do afterwards was to go back to our hotel rooms and take a long, hot bath! I pitched great during the spring because I was mentally and physically prepared to do so. I must admit that the White Sox definitely worked with the pitchers on and off the field. The pitchers would meet three times a week, after dinner, to discuss strategies and study pitching tactics. Compared to what I experienced on other teams, the White Sox had the best bible study! I had the wonderful opportunity to meet some great people who strengthened my belief in Christ. Spring training that year strengthened my entire life! It also helped me deal with my attitude towards life and ignorant people, especially when those people had some influence on or could control my destiny.

After working out all spring in the AAA League, the organization came up with the idea of me becoming the closing pitcher. I'm sure that it had a lot to do with my velocity, which was ninety-two to ninety-four miles per hour. My velocity just kept picking up each year. It may have had something to do with my training or my anger and frustration within. I was assigned back to an AA ball club, the Birmingham Barons. I was told what my role would be, and what was expected of me. I went there without any fuss, but with this killer instinct. They had a brand new stadium, and boy was it beautiful! The locker rooms were larger than most Major League locker rooms. This was my first time as a reliever since my first year of professional baseball. My pitching coach helped

 Dreams Do Exist

me mentally prepare myself. The key was to terminate anything that was in my way. I worked for six saves out of eight tries. My determination, velocity and control opened some eyes and ears. Some of the brass came to town to see me pitch. After I pitched in relief two straight games, the farm director and general manager told me that I was going back to Chicago with them. On the third day that I was given the ball to pitch, I gave up three hits and two runs. Management decided to leave for Chicago without me!

All I thought about was being so close but yet so far away from reaching my ultimate goal. One of the organizations top prospects was struggling in the AAA League and was sent down to AA ball. We were both competing for the same title, and I was switched to long relief and the new arrival was given the closing spot. I knew that I was doing the job, and doing it well. It hurt to watch someone struggling in a job that I knew I was doing very well. All I could do was pray. I knew that I had no control over the organization's decisions. I was still hoping to be called up in September.

When the season ended, I had some pretty good numbers. However, I was not called up and even though my companion struggled; he was still given another chance in the Major Leagues. That did not stop my desire to reach my ultimate goal! I didn't understand what the organization was doing. In my mind however, my destiny was in God's hands. With the season behind me, I returned home. At the age of twenty-eight, I felt as though I was mature enough to commit myself in marriage to my girlfriend of two years. I got married during the off season. We had no plans of having children anytime soon because I saw how difficult it was to have a family while playing in the Minor Leagues. It was tough both mentally and physically to have a family in professional sports. Even though some people do it, it was never in my plans.

Off-Season 1988

Off-season '88 was pretty much the same as off-season '87. I continued to sell used cars and worked out with the Towson State's baseball team. Having a wife felt like having another full time job. I couldn't wait for spring training to begin!

Spring Training 1989 & Rehabilitation

This spring was very important for me because I was injured on the first day of workouts while throwing on the side. It was a pretty nasty day. It was raining and lightning. Because of the weather, practice had been scheduled for the afternoon. By the time we got the opportunity to throw, it was late in the afternoon. I slipped and pulled my pronator, the muscle that controls the rotation of your arm. When it happened, it felt like someone was holding fire to the side of my arm. The trainer put an ice bag on my arm and told me to ice my arm again later that night. It took at least 3 weeks before I could throw again, and when I did throw the pain came right back and I re-injured it. I was told that I would be okay, not to worry. This was coming from the farm director and general manager.

I didn't see a doctor until the second time that I injured my arm. The doctor said I pulled a muscle. At the time I was on the AAA roster. Teams were ready to break to go to their destination, so I was supposed to stay in spring training for an extended period until my arm healed. Instead, my farm director told me that he was going to try and trade me to another team. I responded that I was still hurt. Further, I said, "If you attempt to trade me, I will let the other team know that I am still hurt." He seemed to get angry with me and then handed me my release papers. I never signed the release papers because legally you can't release a player who is hurt, and I requested to see a doctor back home in Baltimore. I wanted to see this particular doctor because in addition to being a doctor for the Orioles, he was also a personal friend of mine.

After being given an M.R.I., the doctors learned that the muscle was slightly torn and I was told that it would take six months of treatment and rehab to heal. There went the season! Even though I would still be paid for the entire season, I really hated to miss being on the field. Rehab was longer than expected. I was in rehab from May until December. To this day I thank God for health insurance. I would not have wanted to pay for that bill. It was thick. No one could have told me that I would play baseball ever again!

The doctor cleared me to go back to work in December. I decided to stop playing baseball and get a real job. However, I needed money to go back to school. I went back to my old job at Montgomery Wards as a security specialist in January. Now that I had a wife and a few more bills, I needed more income than Montgomery Wards could provide. I had to take on a part time job as well, and it was very tough. I still had to find some time to work out here and there. I'm glad that I made the time to work out because in late March one of my farm directors from way back, Mr. Joe Klein called me and asked me, "How is that arm?" "Fine I guess." I replied. Joe said that he had lost quite a few pitchers. He went on to say that he could sure use some help. I talked it over with the wife and against her decision; I decided to give it one more try. After all, money was tight and it was something that I had to do. God is so very good, and I'm sure that it was his way of rewarding me for all that I've done for baseball.

When I arrived to Hanes City, Florida, there was just about two weeks of spring training left. Within eight days, I was pitching in an inter-squad game. I pitched well, but my arm was killing me. Every day that I pitched, I was running back to the dorm to ice my arm. While other guys were playing golf, fishing and going out at night, I would be in my room doing something to my arm. As the teams left camp for their destinations, I stayed back in extended spring training until the cold weather broke. One month later I was feeling great and was sent to Memphis, Tennessee to play AA baseball. I didn't feel any pain and pitched great! I was then promoted to AAA baseball. Not only was I happy about the promotion, I was even more excited to find out that I was going to be a father in January.

1990 Season – Memphis to Omaha

At one point we posted a 6-0 record with a 2.13 E.R.A. The team was already in first place and I just helped to put a cap on it. I became the number one starter for the team finishing the season with a record of 6-2 with a 3.21 E.R.A. I was given the first start of the playoffs and pitched eight strong innings. We won that game. I was then given the ball to pitch the final game of the AAA classic. The game was played in Omaha, the site of the College World Series. The game was against the Rochester Redwings, a Baltimore Orioles affiliate. I pitched seven innings with no walks, three hits and eleven strikeouts. During the game a teammate told me that I had a chance to break the record for strikeouts in a play-off game. The current record was eleven strikeouts. I had ten strikeouts after six innings. I recorded one more in the seventh inning before I was lifted from the game. I thought that my manager Sal Rende took me out of the game because he thought if I broke the record, I was surely headed to the Major Leagues! We won not only that game but the entire series. We shared champagne, celebrations, tears, and the television spotlight. Even with this victory, I felt as though my dream would never become reality. So without a bit of patience in my bones, I went to my apartment packed all my belongings and headed for home. It was one of my fastest and sloppiest departures ever! I drove eighteen hours stopping only for gas. I cried until I reached my door in Baltimore City.

After being given an M.R.I., the doctors learned that the muscle was slightly torn and I was told that it would take six months of treatment and rehab to heal. There went the season! Even though I would still be paid for the entire season, I really hated to miss being on the field. Rehab was longer than expected. I was in rehab from May until December. To this day I thank God for health insurance. I would not have wanted to pay for that bill. It was thick. No one could have told me that I would play baseball ever again!

The doctor cleared me to go back to work in December. I decided to stop playing baseball and get a real job. However, I needed money to go back to school. I went back to my old job at Montgomery Wards as a security specialist in January. Now that I had a wife and a few more bills, I needed more income than Montgomery Wards could provide. I had to take on a part time job as well, and it was very tough. I still had to find some time to work out here and there. I'm glad that I made the time to work out because in late March one of my farm directors from way back, Mr. Joe Klein called me and asked me, "How is that arm?" "Fine I guess." I replied. Joe said that he had lost quite a few pitchers. He went on to say that he could sure use some help. I talked it over with the wife and against her decision; I decided to give it one more try. After all, money was tight and it was something that I had to do. God is so very good, and I'm sure that it was his way of rewarding me for all that I've done for baseball.

When I arrived to Hanes City, Florida, there was just about two weeks of spring training left. Within eight days, I was pitching in an inter-squad game. I pitched well, but my arm was killing me. Every day that I pitched, I was running back to the dorm to ice my arm. While other guys were playing golf, fishing and going out at night, I would be in my room doing something to my arm. As the teams left camp for their destinations, I stayed back in extended spring training until the cold weather broke. One month later I was feeling great and was sent to Memphis, Tennessee to play AA baseball. I didn't feel any pain and pitched great! I was then promoted to AAA baseball. Not only was I happy about the promotion, I was even more excited to find out that I was going to be a father in January.

1990 Season – Memphis to Omaha

At one point we posted a 6-0 record with a 2.13 E.R.A. The team was already in first place and I just helped to put a cap on it. I became the number one starter for the team finishing the season with a record of 6-2 with a 3.21 E.R.A. I was given the first start of the playoffs and pitched eight strong innings. We won that game. I was then given the ball to pitch the final game of the AAA classic. The game was played in Omaha, the site of the College World Series. The game was against the Rochester Redwings, a Baltimore Orioles affiliate. I pitched seven innings with no walks, three hits and eleven strikeouts. During the game a teammate told me that I had a chance to break the record for strikeouts in a play-off game. The current record was eleven strikeouts. I had ten strikeouts after six innings. I recorded one more in the seventh inning before I was lifted from the game. I thought that my manager Sal Rende took me out of the game because he thought if I broke the record, I was surely headed to the Major Leagues! We won not only that game but the entire series. We shared champagne, celebrations, tears, and the television spotlight. Even with this victory, I felt as though my dream would never become reality. So without a bit of patience in my bones, I went to my apartment packed all my belongings and headed for home. It was one of my fastest and sloppiest departures ever! I drove eighteen hours stopping only for gas. I cried until I reached my door in Baltimore City.

When I arrived, my wife was in bed. Since I didn't alert her to the fact that I was on my way home, she was surprised by my arrival. I just crawled into bed without saying a word and feel asleep. A few hours later, my wife awakened me for a phone call. It was the Royal's general manager, Joe Klein. Joe congratulated me on the game that I had just pitched. "Thank you," I replied. Joe then asked me, "What are you doing at home?" I didn't understand his question. Joe said, "Congratulations, you're a Major Leaguer." I couldn't believe my ears! I simply said, "Thank you, Jesus." Joe asked, "When can you get here?" I said, "I'll be there tonight."

We immediately booked a flight to Minnesota. I made it to the hotel before the team arrived from Oakland. When the team arrived in Minnesota, my roommate walked in and called my name before he could see my face. I knew his voice. It was Terry Shumpert. He congratulated me on making it to the Majors. I couldn't sleep for two days. It was a four game series and I was scheduled to possibly pitch when we returned to Kansas City. During batting practice, I got the opportunity to shake hands with Kirby Puckett, Shane Mack and some other players. My first pitching coach from the Texas Rangers organization also con-gratulated me. He was now the pitching coach for the Minnesota Twins. He had helped me out a long time ago when I was 6'1", 165 lbs. and pitching like Sachel Paige.

The last game in Minnesota while I was getting in some bullpen work at the end of the game, the pitcher who was in the game could not record the final two outs. The bullpen phone rang, and then someone asked me, "Are you loose?" "Yeah, why?" I replied. He replied, "You're going in." As my knees started shak-ing I watched John Whathen signal for me to enter the game. I was pumped up. Flawless in mechanics, my first batter was Ken Herbeck and just as quick as I released my first pitch, I watched it soar about four hundred feet! As I watched the ball, I knew it was going to be foul. Someone from the dugout said, "Get that pitch down." I did as requested and recorded my first out, a fly ball to Bo Jackson in left field. My first pitching opportunity in the majors left me with a great feeling! After the game we showered and got on a private plane headed for Kansas City.

When we arrived in Kansas City, Willie Wilson offered me a ride. I smiled as his limousine pulled up. I immediately noticed that is was a real limo and not like the one from my rookie days. Willie also invited me to stay at his home for the first home stand. To this day I'm still thankful for Willie opening his home to me. I didn't get a chance to pitch in Kansas City but I did start the final game of the season in Cleveland. In that game I pitched almost six innings before leaving the game ahead two to one with men on first and second. We ended up losing the game 3 to 2. It was the last game of the season and it was a day game. After the game, I flew straight to Baltimore from Cleveland. Later that night I was watching the Orioles play their final game. It felt weird because while I was at the Orioles game, it was announced that I was the losing pitcher in the Cleveland game. Nobody knew that I was in the stands, except my buddy Mike a long time usher at Memorial Stadium. Things are so much nicer in the Major Leagues. There is such a difference in the type of travel, the food, the hotels and even buses in the Majors compared to the Minor League! However, you must work harder to stay in the Majors when you get there.

1990 Winter Ball - Maracay, Venezuela

During the off season, management sent me to winter ball to work on my slider. The pay for winter ball is good, but it takes you away from your family. Too much time away from your family can cause problems. After two and a half months in Venezuela, I was ready to get back to the United States. Several players got sick mostly with digestive problems. Living in Venezuela wasn't too bad since I speak Spanish; dealing with the fans was another story. There were many fans that bet on the games. This would affect their reactions

to a lost, or when they saw a terrible play. Ice, mangoes, oranges, and apples were among the things that were thrown on the field. Bottles were even tossed on the field. Crime was everywhere.

One day while playing in Venezuela we had a team fight and a few guys got hurt. The next day, during batting practice I actually saw a player with a 38 revolver clamped to his baseball pants. That was all I had to see to keep me from throwing a punch at someone. Team fights in Mexico and other foreign countries truly get out of hand.

Happy that we didn't make the playoffs in winter ball, I was fortunate enough to make it home to attend some Lamaze classes before the baby arrived. I saved up enough money from winter ball, so I didn't have to work for the next two months. I was told that I would be invited to Major League spring training. I worked out for the next two months at Towson State until spring arrived. While I was home, my daughter, Taylor Monei Smith was born.

Season 1991 - Omaha

It was a very trying and disappointing year for me. It came with some of my life's most challenging decisions. After being assigned back to Omaha, Nebraska to play AAA ball with the Royals, I now had to travel with a wife and newborn. This was something that I always tried to avoid at the Minor League level. I had just finished my first spring training on the Major League level, and it was one of my best ever!

My family and I arrived in Omaha around April 3rd. Within 3 days we had to find an apartment and furnish it. If we did not find an apartment, we would be forced to live in the hotel until we found an apartment. After the season started, I was very excited about being with my family for the first time ever during regular season. It was also great to watch my daughter grow up around me.

The season opened at home in Omaha. After the opening, we were scheduled for road games for the next twelve days. I was the third to start this year. This was disappointing since I had been the best pitcher last year during the regular season and during tournament play. After returning from the road, my wife told me that she would rather be near her mother and sisters in Florida. It was hard to swallow that I would be away from my family again.

After four starts, I was one and one with two no decisions. During our third road trip to Denver, it was still early in the season and very cold. Unfortunately for me, I had to pitch in near freezing weather and as a result, I ended up pulling an oblique abdominal muscle. I was placed on the disabled list for sixty days.

Missing those two months of the season truly ended my chances of an early promotion or of any promotion at all. I did return to the team, but I finished the season, with an E.R.A. of 3.52, with five wins and two losses. My one hundred strikeouts to thirty-three walks didn't even help me for a September call up. However, it was still fun season! My two best friends on the team were Jacob Brumfield and Jeffery (Hac Man) Lenard, who both also had a very good season. Jeffery treated Jacob and I like family. He also knew that we were very talented, and advised Jacob and I to never stop chasing our dream. After the season, Jacob and I drove my truck to Kansas City. We stopped in the office of the Kansas City Royals and spoke with Joe Klein. Joe advised us on what we needed to do to reach the Major League level. That same day I drove Jacob home to Atlanta and spent the night at his home. The next morning, I left for Florida to be with my wife and daughter. After arriving in Florida things didn't get any better with my wife. Winter ball in the Dominican Republic didn't happen, as my marriage was in serious trouble. I worked eight hours a day at Broward County Juvenile Detention Center mentoring youth and played softball three nights a week. The American dream of be-

ing a full time husband and father had vanished, as my marriage ended. I was still very proud to be a father.

Spring 1992 – Milan, Italy

At the end of the season, I was contacted by Mario Mazzotta, one of the managers of the Medialono baseball club in Italy. Mario expressed great interest in my playing on the Medialono baseball club for the 1992 season. At first I was very uncertain because I was pretty sure that I was going to be called up again with the Royals. At the end of the season my record was four wins, five loses, eight no decisions, ninety-four strikeouts, thirty-three walks with a 3.24 E.R.A. However, a lot of things started going wrong for me after my last start in the Major Leagues. Actually it was my only start in the Major Leagues! It was suggested that I spend the winter in Venezuela and work on a third pitch. My stay was very short in the Major Leagues because I ended up getting walking pneumonia and had to return home. I did not receive a contract in either the Major or Minor Leagues, after a pretty good Minor League AAA season, with the Omaha Royals. I decided to spend the next season in Italy playing baseball.

After working at Broward Juvenile Detention Center in Florida, I asked for a leave of absence to continue my career in the Italian baseball league. I made this decision for a couple of reasons. First, I was going through a divorce and needed the extra money. Second, it was a great opportunity to see a place I was not naturally inclined to visit!

I went by the Yankee spring camp to see Danny Tartabull, we played together for the Kansas City Royals. I mentioned to Danny that I was preparing to leave for Italy in a week to play in the Italian baseball league. Danny asked me if I would be willing to speak with the general manager of the Yankees before leaving the American baseball league. After speaking with the Yankees General

Manager, Gene Michael, I found myself on the mound pitching under the watchful eye of the pitching coach and manager Buck Shoewalter. They must have been pleased with what they saw, because afterwards they talked and then the general manager called me in his office and offered me an invitation to Major League spring training. I told Gene that I had an offer to play baseball in Italy. Gene thought that I should stay and try my luck in the Major Leagues one more time. I knew that this was a chance of a lifetime, but I also knew that I had earned the right to tryout!

Gene told me to take a few days to think it over. I returned to the Yankee clubhouse two days before I was supposed to leave for Italy. First I talked to Danny while he was hitting in the batting cage. He reminded me that the decision I was about to make could change my life. He also shared with me that the caliber of baseball in Italy was in no comparison to here in the states. I thanked Danny for the advice. I then went to Gene's office. I had my daughter Taylor with me. As I was about to enter Gene's office, a reporter stopped me and asked if I had brought my daughter with me as a lucky charm. "No." I replied. It was just one of those days when I had full responsibility for my daughter. That meant wherever I went, she went also!
Reporters can be so insensitive at times.

As Gene and I talked, he was only able to offer an invitation to spring training camp with no incentives in case I did not make the Major League club. I told him that I would be up a creek if I turned down the offer with the Italian League, and didn't make the Yankee team. Gene asked if I would consider staying a couple of weeks while getting every opportunity to pitch. I told him that I would have to get permission from the manager of Medialono's Baseball Club. Gene allowed me to call him from his office. I told Mario Mazzotta about the opportunity that I had with the Yankees. Mario reminded me that he was depending on me to pitch this year for him. He also cautioned me that he couldn't wait two weeks to know whether he would be left without an American pitcher. After talking to Mario Mazzotta again, the next day I decided to go for the money, and play in the Italian League. Gene wished me luck and told me to stay in touch.

On the flight I was talking to this young lady who lived in Iran. We talked about our respective countries. She talked about what her country was like during the midst of war. She was grateful that her family had not been directly affected by the war. Nonetheless, she said it was still pretty scary. After an eleven-hour flight, I made it to Italy. That was the longest flight I had ever taken in my life. Milan made a great first impression! There was lots of press at the airport for me and another American named Jim Walewonder. His wife, Ann, accompanied him. We flew over on the same flight and didn't even recognize each other until we landed in Milan.

When I arrived at my apartment at 31 Via Cabelea Street in Milan, everyone was looking at me. To be more exact, they were actually staring. Italy is six hours ahead of the eastern coast of the United States. After I got used to the time change, I caught my second wind and finally took my first trip to downtown Milan to the baseball team's office. Milan reminded me of New York City. There were apartments on top of apartments. There were cars parked on the sidewalks, and there was lots of traffic.

Later that day some staff members dropped off my car. It was a 1990 white Fiat. The car was mine for the duration of my stay in Milan. My contract included an apartment, a car and money for meals when the team was on the road. All I had to pay for was gas for the car and my telephone bill. My first day of practice was wild. We practiced outside in the cold under a huge tent. Some of the guys on my team could speak English, but most could not. Practice wasn't bad except for the frigid cold weather. After practice, twenty minutes of jogging really warmed me up. I slept like a baby that night. Basically, all we did was practice all week. We ate lots of pasta.

One day I decided to venture out in my Fiat to try and learn my way around town and to find a supermarket. Of course, I got lost a few times. I had to be very careful on the roads as the Italians drove as if there were no traffic rules! On the other hand, shopping for food really wasn't that bad. My apartment was furnished, so I had everything that I needed. Cooking was easy as long as I was cooking for myself.

Our first game was pretty exciting for me because I faced guys who used aluminum bats. We won our first game and lost the second one the next day. Overall it was an exciting season. We stayed in second place. Prior to coming to Italy, I wasn't familiar with any of the players in the Italian League. It was good to discover that some of the players were really very good ball players. Jim, the other American player and I became good friends. We did a lot of traveling together while in Italy. Roberto Beanci, an Italian player and I also became good friends. Roberto was consistently the home run leader on the team. We went out to clubs together and he taught me how to fish for trout. He was so funny. Every time he caught a trout, he would hit it on the head with the knob of his screwdriver and yell "Morto!", which means dead. Roberto also gave me some Italian literature to practice my Italian. Prior to giving me the literature, he gave me a private lesson teaching me some dirty words. I actually learned how to speak the language pretty well. Italian and Spanish are very similar, and I studied Spanish while in school. I also learned a lot of the language from playing and spending time with the Italian players.

Our road trips were pretty pleasant because we had a very nice bus. We watched movies while en route to play. Since we only

played two games a week it was important to at least win the first game. During the first game, the non-Italian players would pitch against each other. During the second game, the Italians would pitch against each other. American pitchers played another position on their off-pitching day. I always pitched. For most games there were nine innings. After the game, we went out for a night on the town. We had lots of fun at the club called Hollywood's. Many Italians also spoke English. Once I became a regular at Hollywood's, my guest and I were treated better than the V.I.P.'s. I used to see the team owner's son at Hollywood's all the time. He was a pretty cool guy. It was rare to see a black woman at Hollywood's. I did meet a black woman at the underground transit station. She mentioned that she had been living in Milan for about three years and that she worked and lived with her boyfriend who was Italian. She hooked me up with some of her friends, and we all hung out a few times.

As the season neared the halfway point, we remained in second place, and our team was in great shape before the break. The break came just before July. The last week of June we flew to the Netherlands to compete in the Italian Super Cup Baseball title, which lasted for about five days. We played pretty good baseball and made it to the finals. Most of the teams were competitive except for the one team from Ireland. They had a lot of young players, and we just smoked them. In fact we were beating them so badly one day that they attempted to injure, Jim Walewonder, the other American player. At that point Jim asked our manager to take him out of the game because he didn't want to get hurt. Our manager refused to take Jim out of the game. Jim simply took himself out of the game and walked back to the hotel in full uniform! The hotel was a good two to three miles from the park. After the game we were on our way back to the hotel, and we passed Jim along the way. The bus did a u-turn and stopped to pick him up. He refused the ride. Jim was my roommate. When he returned to the hotel, I asked him, "Why did it take you so long to get back to the hotel? You left the game in the top of the third inning." I continued. Jim told me that he stopped and took a nap on the soccer field until this guy told him to move on. I shared with him that we won the game nineteen to one!

Before the last day of the series, we had a day off. On our off day, I went with some of my teammates to Amsterdam by train. It was only thirty minutes away. On the train to Amsterdam, we were sitting behind two guys who actually were exchanging marijuana out in the open. After I mentioned it to one of my teammates, he told me that it was legal! I quickly learned that just about everything was legal in Amsterdam. We had a great time that day! It was around 8:00 p.m. when we headed back to the hotel. Most of us turned in for the night. We had to win two games the next day.

The next morning we had to play against the Brazilians who were undefeated. We had to win two games against the Brazilians to be champions of the Italian Super Cups Tournament. I was scheduled to pitch the first game. I pitched nine innings only giving up two hits. We won seven to zero! We prepared for the second game, which was scheduled to begin at 1:00 p.m. I was icing my shoulder, as the second game began. We were playing pretty good into the eighth inning. At that point we were trailing 3 to 2. By the eighth inning we had used all six of our Italian pitchers. The current pitcher, Raul, an Italian star pitcher, was currently in the game and had gotten into a little jam. He was currently in a heated argument with the home plate umpire over a very critical call. After the argument, Raul was tossed from the game. Team management then came to me and asked me to pitch. I said, "You're joking, right?" "No", my manager said, "I'm quite serious. We don't have any other pitchers. You're the only one left, and we need to win this game to be champs" he continued. Before I knew it, one of the players had taken my spikes out of my bag, and

Dreams Do Exist

placed them at my feet. I was still in disbelief. He started untying my turf shoes and putting on my spikes. Another teammate was trying to put my jersey on over top of my jacket. I said to myself "This is crazy." as I looked at my teammate Jim for help. Jim just shrugged his shoulders. I strapped on my gear and took the pitcher's mound. There was one out, with men at first and third bases. I took about five pitches to warm up and said "Let's go". Heck, I figured if I wasn't loose by now, I would never be loose. With two pitches we were out of the inning with a 6-4-3 double play. In the bottom of the eighth inning we rallied for two runs, which put us on top of the home team 4 to 3. As I took the mound for the bottom of the 9th inning, I couldn't believe the energy that I had. Striking out the first two batters and getting the third out from a ground ball to shortstop, we won the Italian Super Cups of '92. The last thing that I remembered was my teammates all piling up on top of me for winning the tournament. After the game I was presented the MOSP Valuable Player Award and the team was presented with the tournament cup. The cup looked like a hockey championship cup, silver and large, with the handles. My award was a silk screen 14 by 11 painting of Don Dreysdale, which was one of only one hundred in the world. It even had a certificate. The next morning I grabbed a paper and my photo was in it holding the silk screen painting over my head. All I could think about was the statistics of my performance that day 10 and 2/3rds innings pitched 2 hits 0 walks and 18 strikeouts.

The plane ride back to Milan was very pleasant with plenty of time to prepare ourselves for the second half of the season. We had the whole month of July off. Instead of going home, the team flew my mother Ruby over to Italy to spend the month with me. My mother and I had a wonderful time together. July is very hot in Italy. Milan along with several other Italian cities were empty because many Italians vacationed during July. Most residents would head south to the beaches. My mom and I didn't stay in Milan for too long, because it was really hot. After showing her around downtown Milan with its art rooms and cathedrals, we decided to spend a week on the road seeing different parts of Italy. We even visited Zurich Switzerland.

Home Plate

Off Season 1992

I returned to Fort Lauderdale, Florida and continued working as a detention childcare worker, helping the troubled youth of Florida. I also was able to spend some well-needed time with my daughter, who was almost two years old! The beautiful weather allowed me to play softball from October to February for three different teams. Living in Florida was great for me not only because it allowed me to spend precious time with my daughter, additionally, the warmer weather allowed me to play baseball even in the off-season!

Fishing at Alligator Alley and the Florida Keys was also enjoyable. This was my second off-season in Fort Lauderdale since I had stopped playing AAA baseball. I took advantage of the chance to take my daughter back home to Baltimore to visit my side of the family, my siblings, Karreen, Michelle, Ruth, and James. It was most important for my daughter to also spend time with my mother, her grandmother Ruby. Taylor enjoyed herself tremendously. She didn't get a chance to meet her great-grandfather who unfortunately died the day before we arrived in Baltimore. I took her with me to the funeral and she met other extended family members.

Mexico 1993

I had plenty of help training and preparing for the upcoming season in Mexico. I worked out at Bally's Scandinavian Health Club in Fort Lauderdale, Florida. I did all of my weight training, swimming and racquetball training there. Additionally, I worked with Dillard High School's baseball team to get in all of my throwing, pitching, and batting practice. While at the high school, it was extremely satisfying for me to work with their young pitchers. My gratitude goes out to Coach Gray and the guys who I played summer softball with, and also to the guys from Hollywood, Florida's amateur hardball team.

 Dreams Do Exist

The team that I signed with in Mexico was named the Mexico City Reds. This team was considered to be the Yankees of Mexico. They were affiliated with the Pittsburgh Pirates AAA franchise. My report date was February 23rd. We worked out for a good two weeks before the team went on the road for two more weeks of exhibition games all over Mexico. We didn't get paid for these games; we just received meal money and hotel accommodations. It was hard to breathe in parts of Mexico because of the altitude. The pollution in Mexico didn't help much either. At times I thought I would just die because breathing was so difficult!

During spring training we played in front of moderate crowds and in some poorly kept ballparks. I can recall traveling by ferry for fifteen minutes to play a team. We had very nice uniforms and the team that we played had homemade uniforms. There was no place to change into and out of your uniform, as the team didn't have locker rooms. After beating one of the Mexican teams, I remember seeing a few ice cubes and bottles tossed onto the field. I only stayed after the game long enough to shake hands before boarding the bus.

The ferry ride back to Cozumel wasn't that bad because of the view. The other fields and cities that we played in weren't much better. We opened the season in front of about twelve thousand fans. The excitement was there but nothing compared to opening day in the United States. Nevertheless, all was going well and I was expecting to see my daughter soon for Easter. On the day that she arrived, one month into the season, I was called to the team's office and released because the owner said that he didn't want a forkballer as a closer anymore. Statistically, I was doing just fine, so the manager and owner opted to find me another team. My Easter weekend wasn't as pleasant as it could have been. I saw my daughter off to the airport after her stay. I waited in Mexico City for a week to be placed on another team. But the team who was interested ended up signing someone else. I said my good-byes to my teammates.

My return to Fort Lauderdale, Florida was sooner than I had expected. Everyone was surprised to see me before the season was over. I had already spoken with the detention center about getting my job back. When my agent called for me to return to Mexico to play for another team, I was still in shape to pitch. One week later, I decided to return to Mexico. This time I would play in Monclova, Mexico, a small city twelve hours away from Mexico City. It seemed as if it was a blessing for me because the conditions were better than in Mexico City. There was only one downside with this team. They had no major affiliate in the United States. Nonetheless, I met some really nice people. I was also reunited with Eddie Castro, Julio Silano, Alex Sanchez, and other players with whom I had played with in the United States. We played 500 baseball and I got the chance to prove to my former team in Mexico City that they should have kept me! One game even resulted in to a bench-clearing shoving match because of my performance. My team played well enough to make the playoffs, but we didn't make it out of the first series. I got a chance to see several parts of Mexico for about five months. I even posted a 12 and 2 record as a starter.

Every town in Mexico was different. Some were large, and some were small. All of them shared the same type of atmosphere. Like every place else, there were rich areas and poverty sections. The two things that I enjoyed most was getting the opportunity to compete against some of Mexico's finest baseball players and getting the chance to see a lot of Mexico's historic sites. I even took home some great hand-made souvenirs for friends and family. I'll never forget the long and dangerous bus rides to and from games!

Off-Season 1993 - 1995

I had already planned to spend the off-season in Baltimore. I shipped my trunk and other personal belongings back. I only kept a few bags with things I needed on a daily basis. When I returned to Baltimore in early August, I turned down an offer from my agent to play AAA for the Indians. I had already contacted the general manager for the Orioles about continuing my baseball career with their organization. Four days later I was given a tryout with the Bay Sox who at the time were playing at Memorial Stadium in Baltimore. They were not playing at home because their new stadium was just being built. I drove to Memorial Stadium to pitch on the side for Mr. Buford, the manager. He informed me that he could use me. He also stated that I would be a starter when the team returned back to Baltimore in two days.

All I could think about was how great it would be to somehow get a chance to play for my hometown team. More important was the possibility of staying in the organization for a few years as Major Leaguer! At the age of thirty three, I didn't know if that dream would ever come true since the majority of players in the Major Leagues are a lot younger than thirty three! So I pitched my heart out and didn't really accomplish anything except press coverage from all the major newspapers in Baltimore City. I even gained a moment of fame in the Oriole magazine! The Bay Sox were trying to gain a spot in the playoffs during the month of August. I contributed all that I could but came up with a 0-1 record with 3 no decisions and a modest E.R.A. All of my performances in August were strong. We made the playoffs but were eliminated.

An article published in the Murray Events the summer of 1993 read:
My Son, A Bird? How proud can a mother be? Look at the wide smile that Ruby Saunders wears since her son, Daryl, made his debut in the Orioles organization, pitching at Memorial Stadium

for the Bay Sox. He pitched eight innings of 4-hit ballgame, striking out seven New Britain Red Sox while walking only one. Daryl was not the pitcher of record since the Bay Sox won the game in the ninth inning after he left the game. But he did his job. He kept them in the game. Keep that up, Daryl, and maybe we'll be seeing you at THE YARD!

Fortunately, trying to find an off-season job didn't come as soon as I anticipated because I was offered a cameo role as a character and stand-in double in the movie "Major League II." About one hundred people auditioned for the roles in the movie. However, I did not have to audition for a role. The casting director attended a couple of our games and gave me an opportunity to be part of one of the teams in the movie. Only six of us from the Bay Sox were automatically accepted. After the teams were selected, we were told that we would be filming at Memorial Stadium, Camden Yard and Harrisburg, Pennsylvania's AA stadium.

When we arrived in Harrisburg for the first day of filming, it was great to put on a uniform just for fun. It was also great not having to worry about my performance on the field. It was a relief not having to worry about being released!

After Charlie Sheen, Tom Berenger, Omar Epps, Dennis Hayesbert, Corbin Bernstein and David Keith, arrived on the set, we had a team meeting with the director of the film, David Ward. We were all briefed on what to expect. We were also told that this would not be an easy process. The director reminded the professional athletes that we would be working with actors and not professional baseball players. It was great to see the way a film was made. It was even more exciting to be in one! Harrisburg's stadium was turned into a wonderful spring training site, with palm trees and billboards as if we were in Florida.

The citizens of Harrisburg got a chance to come out and sup-

 Dreams Do Exist

port the making of this film. People piled in by the thousands each day of filming for about one week. I stayed in Harrisburg while we were filming to save myself from commuting each day. I was already familiar with the city of Harrisburg because I played against the local team for a couple of years during part of my minor league stint in the eastern league. Every morning before filming there was plenty of food. We were served breakfast, lunch and dinner and snacks. The catering service that was used was excellent! After completing the filming of spring training in Harrisburg, the movie set moved to Baltimore. Camden Yards was used as the home field for the Cleveland Indians and Memorial Stadium was used as the site of all the road games. I was very fortunate to get a chance to spend time with some very fine actors. Steve Yager played himself and helped choreograph the on-field play. As the stand in for Dennis Hayesbert, I was on the field at all times. Since my arm was still in great shape from the end of the season with the Bay Sox, I was given yet another extra duty to throw all the pitches for Charlie Sheen's pitching performances in the movie.

When I wasn't needed on the set, I was inside the visiting team's locker room at Camden Yards, sleeping, watching television, playing cards or playing video games. We sometimes spent ten to twelve hours on the set. I got to be really good friends with Dennis Hayesbert and Omar Epps, and I can't forget my joke buddy, Tom Berenger. Tom and I used to laugh a lot, and Dennis would occasionally hang out at my apartment or we would go down to the local pool hall to shoot pool. I even went fishing with Eric Bruskotter (a former actor on the show Cheers).
By the end of November the film was just about completed. Central Casting threw a great party when the film was completed. All of the actors, crew and extras were invited. I still stay in touch with Dennis Hayesbert and Tom Berenger.
After vacationing in Fort Lauderdale, Florida with my girlfriend

and my daughter, I returned to Baltimore and took a job at Youth Services International (YSI) as a Juvenile Counselor. YSI is a juvenile detention center. I worked there from December 1993 to February 1995. I also worked for a firm called Justice Resources as an advocate for troubled youngsters who were living at home. While working at the YSI, I did my best to help these youngsters turn their lives around during their incarceration. They attended school and participated in all types of special counseling sessions. In addition to the group counseling, the youngsters were taught personal hygiene, how to deal with peer pressure, and how to constructively solve problems. They also were exposed to all types of sports programs. We even had job fairs for them! While working with Justice Resources I would take my clients out for sporting events and to the movies. I truly felt that my calling was to give back to the community what was given to me when I was growing up as a child. Times are definitely harder now for kids than it was when I was growing up.

I was still hoping to get an invitation to spring training in 1994 with the Baltimore Orioles minor or major league ball clubs. Instead I received my release from the Orioles' system. At the age of 33 it seemed evident that I probably wouldn't receive another job offer. I contacted several ball clubs but I didn't have any success. I did receive an offer to return to Mexico to play for the team that I played for in 1993. My report date was February 20th. An unexpected family crisis canceled any hopes for a 1994 season.

I turned 34 years of age and was pretty much content with the thirteen years of baseball I played in the United States and my two years of baseball abroad. As you may remember the 1994 baseball season was shortened because of the strike. Like most of America, I was pretty distressed without baseball.

Back to the Game

In January of 1995, I received a phone call from a very good friend Curt. He informed me that the New York Yankees had called the detention center trying to find me. Fortunately, Curt had my telephone number and he gave it to them. I then received a call from the Yankees General Manager, Gene Michael. He asked if I was interested in signing a AAA contract. I knew that the strike was still in effect so I saw no harm in going to the Minor Leagues. This would give me a shot at my Major League dreams. This opportunity also included a $10,000.00 signing bonus. I accepted the offer and started preparing for spring training.

I truly signed on hoping that the strike would end because I was promised a shot at the Majors if the strike ended. I guess everybody plays the fool sometimes. I worked out every day for a month and a half while still working at Youth Services International. I gave up the Advocate position with Justice Resources. I was in pretty good condition after training for a month and a half. I was already in great pitching condition and physically I was in good shape from playing basketball, racquetball and jogging.

I decided to leave the cold weather two weeks early and head to Florida. I couldn't stand pitching off of my homemade pitching mounds any longer. Fortunately, I got a couple of opportunities to work out with the Towson State baseball team. When I arrived in Florida, I still had two weeks before my actual report date. I decided to spend some quality time with my daughter. I also used this time to work out again with Coach Gray and the Dillard High School baseball team.

When I arrived at spring training, there was plenty of media and familiar faces. After talking to some old friends, and meeting some of the new guys, I found out that some players had experiences similar to mine in the Minor League and international baseball. In fact, several of the players had been in sales like I was when I wasn't playing baseball. It was very weird, having a Major League owner like George Steinbrenner at spring training. However, because of the baseball strike, most coaches had plenty of time on their hands. We were informed that everything would go on as planned until the strike ended. The question was asked, "What happens when the strike ends?" We were told that some of us would return home and some of us will carry on with our baseball careers.

We started spring training by taking physicals and eye exams. Afterwards, all the players took the field for practice. There were about one hundred fans hanging around the stadium. Reporters were talking to players about their reasons for being here and about their interest in the strike. Some guys looked at the strike as the chance of a lifetime. Others were at spring training just for the money. I never expected the strike to go as far as it did. One night while watching the news, I heard that the union considered everyone who was currently playing baseball as scabs. I thought it was unfair because it wasn't the Minor Leaguers fault that the strike had taken place. What could I say or do. I was up a creek either way, so I continued to play the game I loved.

Our pitching coach, Billy Connors would constantly remind some pitchers that they would probably get a chance to try out for the Major League club. Reporters continued to ask me questions about how I viewed the strike. I just kept my mouth shut and did what the Yankee's staff asked me to do. With less than a week to go before the start of the regular season, several Minor Leaguers started returning to spring training. They were all guaranteed salaries and a job for the season. They were also told that nothing would be held against them. My contract was not guaranteed, but fortunately I was pitching good enough not to need a guarantee. I had twenty-five innings with thirty-one strikeouts and six walks.

I was projected to start either first or second, if the season took place with replacement players.

I must admit after taking team photos and loading up to go to Houston and Denver, I did become a little worried and skeptical about whether or not the strike would end. When we arrived in Houston to play the Astros, I was switched from starter to reliever. I pitched two scoreless innings, bringing my spring training total innings to twenty-seven. Everyone knew something was about to happen because we were using alias names before our last names. Talk of the strike ending was getting louder. We continued our road trip onto Denver. It was a great feeling to be the first to have played at Coors field, the new stadium for the Colorado Rockies. To be present for the ribbon cutting ceremonies and the sellout crowd at the new stadium is something that I will never forget! The fans didn't care who was there. They all came out to be a part of all the excitement.

The day of our last game in Denver, one of my teammates, Matt Starkes informed everyone that the strike had ended and that we all should enjoy our last game. Matt even started placing some of his baseball items like his jocks, shoes, cup, hat, jersey, gloves and other belongings in front of his locker in the Denver locker room with a for-sale sign. I had to laugh and take a picture.

The roster for the next game was supposed to be made the next day before traveling to Texas. We never saw another roster. We spent an extra night in Denver before returning to Fort Lauderdale, Florida. The team put us up for the night and we all had to report to the field the next morning. Some players left from Denver to go home.

When I returned to Florida, I spent the afternoon playing with my daughter. The next morning I reported to the field and was assigned to Columbus, Ohio's AAA ball club with several other players like the Cy Young and MVP winner Willie Hernandez, even though he was forty four years of age! The media was everywhere once again and covered the story about me being assigned to AAA. I left the next morning for Ohio.

Season at Columbus, OH to Mexico

I was the fourth starter in Columbus. Our first four workouts were frigid! You could hardly feel your skin. After practice, we had a team meeting and were told not to discuss the strike or to criticize anyone about the strike. We were informed that Mr. Steinbrenner would take personal actions toward anyone who violated this request. I pitched well but never got a win in seven starts. I was 0-3 with four no decisions. As a starter, I owned the best E.R.A. of 2.90. I even pitched a two-hitter and a one-hitter and lost both games. I guess it just wasn't meant to be. After the Major League level started moving guys around, I was first placed in the bullpen and by June 6th released.

Before I was released, I had a run in with a couple of teammates about pitching in the spring training games. I handled it without knocking anybody's teeth out. Furthermore I wasn't going to let my thirteen-year career be criticized by two people whose years combined totaled less than mine! By June 20th I was playing baseball in Mexico. Before I left the Yankees, I was given $10,000.00 for all my troubles.

I called many American teams before agreeing to play again in Mexico. However, no team in the United States would give me a job. Mexico was my third stop for the 1995 season. I figured since I was still healthy, what the heck. I played in Mexico for almost three months. The Mexican teams were also affected by the Major League strike.

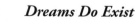

I played for a team in the Saltilo mountains, the Sarraperos. We played very well until the playoffs came. We lost in five games in the playoffs. I pitched the fourth game and won. While playing there I met a player who had some connections in Taiwan and was offered a job. I returned to Baltimore on August 2nd and spent time with my family for two weeks. During that time I acquired my visa so that I could head for Taiwan.

Season in Taiwan

Taiwan was a very good experience for me. The flight was sixteen hours and the culture and food are definitely different. They also have some strange ways of getting around the city. Taiwan has bumper to bumper traffic everywhere. I couldn't believe my eyes when we first came to the city. There were people everywhere! There were many cars but definitely more scooters than cars. People were also riding bikes, riding carts and pushing vending carts. This was far different than anything that I have ever seen before in my life! There are a few modern stores and restaurants there like 7-Eleven, Circle K, Wendy's, McDonald's and Fridays. But there were far more self-operated and Chinese-owned food stands and stores there. Open-air food stands were very popular.

Most of the stands had food that we would usually only see during a festival or fair, in the United States. However, in Taiwan, this type of food was available every day. The food was different than what I was used to seeing and eating. Sure, I would prefer soul food or just a good home-cooked meal from my mom. However, you have to choose from what's available. The choice between eating Taiwanese food from an American food chain became easy for me. I would have to spend about twenty-four dollars round trip by taxi to get American fast food, but after I describe some of the choices, I'm sure that you would want to make the trip. The food in the open-air carts is uncovered. The carts carried everything from ground beef, baked chicken, fried chicken, hotdogs, beef sticks, sausage, squid on a stick, and I can't forget the bird on a stick. They also offered hard boiled pigeon eggs. One of my teammates tried to convince me that pigeon eggs tasted like eggs from a chicken. He suggested that I try them. I declined his offer. According to my teammates, some people even eat dog meat. Dog meat was supposed to extend your life span. I sure hope that wasn't what I ate in my fried rice.

At the ballpark there was plenty of food available. Unlike at American stadiums, there were lots of noodles, bread, pork dumplings, sushi, rice and vegetables. I ate lots of rice, noodles and veggies.

I'm also amazed that the players would eat just before a game. The games didn't last as long as they do in Mexico, thank God. The games were fast and the players were pretty good. The hardest part was adapting to their style of play. The same was true in Mexico, Italy and Venezuela. If you were American, you were at a disadvantage because the umpires usually favored the native players. You didn't get a lot of strikes called as a American pitcher and the strike zone got very big when an American was hitting. It was tough enough striking a player out with three strikes. However, Taiwanese players would be allowed about four or five strikes from time to time.

The stadiums in Taiwan are small and the baseball fields were in need of improvement. The fans are very loud and most are very friendly. Baseball fans show their excitement in different ways. They bang on drums, blow air horns, chant together and bang cones together while their team is batting. Every game has a most valuable player, who receives a trophy. Every game is televised and the female fans bring flowers to their favorite players. Each team is allowed ten non-Taiwanese players.

In 1995, baseball had professionally been in existence for six years in Taiwan and there were six teams. Each team was named after an animal. They had the Elephants, the Lions, the Tigers, the Bears, the Eagles and the Dragons. Two of the teams were amateur teams. Each team had its own customized bus with the team's name and logo on it. Baseball in Taiwan offered all sorts of cash bonuses. If you pitched a complete game shut out, you would earn $1,000.00 U.S. dollars. Winning the batting title would earn you about $16,000.00 U.S. dollars. If you led the league in home runs, wins or stolen bases you could garner $12,000 U.S. to $16,000 U.S. dollars.

Ron Jones, a friend of mine was tied for the home-run title with twenty-three home runs. He was tied with a Taiwanese player with one game to go. The next game he was intentionally walked four times and they allowed the Taiwanese player to hit a home run so that he could win the cash. Ron was ticked off!

In Taiwan you can negotiate a contract where no taxes are taken from your paycheck. Because the season is so long, you are paid all year round. The baseball season lasts for ten months. Players have November and December off, and they return for spring training in January. Once spring training began, you would be paid for November and December. If you didn't mind being away from your family, Taiwan was definitely the place to make some extra cash!

In 1996 I planned on returning to Taiwan for my final season of baseball. My contract was valid until October 31st 1995, but my visa ended on the 27th of October. After three days of negotiations, I signed a big contract for 1996. Spring training was held in Australia. After spring training, the flight back to the states took seventeen hours! It took me one week to get over the jet lag. Once I recovered, I was off to visit my daughter in Florida. When

I returned two weeks later, I started work again as a youth counselor at my previous employer.

In mid-January, I was more than happy to leave for Australia since there was a foot of snow in Baltimore. Once I arrived in Australia, we worked out twice daily, which was a little hard on my body. I was able to travel a bit while I was in Australia. I was able to visit the Gold coast before we left for another month of training in Taiwan.

There were plenty of distractions before the season even started. We lost a player from last year, because of our new General Manager. China was launching missiles at Taiwan just over our heads while we were preparing for the season. It was a very threatening situation. China didn't want Taiwan to become an independent nation. They tried to stop their elections from taking place. When the Chinese aggression intensified, I felt as though it was time for me to go. I sent my mom an article about the situation. She had one question for me after reading the article. "Do you need a plane ticket home?" She asked.

I told her "Mom, don't worry, we are being guarded by the U S. S. Nimitz. Somehow, that answer didn't seem to settle her nerves. I thought about it a little longer and decided to follow my mother's advice and return home. I honestly knew that it was time to say goodbye to baseball.

Life Goes On

The plane ride home was a little somber and I didn't tell anyone except my girlfriend that I was coming home. I came back frustrated, tired and uncertain of my relationship with my girlfriend. I decided to take a vacation to Fort Lauderdale, Florida to relax and to clear my mind. I was also looking forward to visiting my daughter.

I went back to the Broward County Detention Center and contacted my co-workers, Mr. Lampkin, Mrs. Graham, Mrs. Outlaw and Mr. Perkins. Over the years we had became very close and I looked forward to us getting together. They truly became my family away from home, especially when I had been going through some difficult times with my ex-wife. When we had a chance to catch up, we talked about my days working at the detention center and how the youth there desperately needed positive role models. There was one kid in particular that was still at the detention center. We referred to him as "the problem child". By the time he was fourteen, he had sixty-seven various charges including burglary and armed robbery. I remember when I first met him in 1991. At that time he was ten years old. He reminded me of my own childhood. I understood how important the support of my family had been to me when I was growing up. I could easily have gone down the wrong path. Motivating these kids was helpful for them and uplifting for me too!

As I reflected on my years in the minor leagues, I was reminded of the many times I thought of giving up and how important it had been for me to see my potential even if it seemed no one around me could see it. At this point I decided that no matter what career path I chose that I would stay involved with mentoring kids. My vacation was over and I returned to Baltimore. Now that I considered myself officially retired from baseball, I went to purchase a car. At the car dealership, I spoke to George Gillium, a friend of mine. He suggested I try car sales as a career path because I had great people skills. I was introduced to the owner, Len Stoler and began working for the dealership in July 1996. I wasn't looking forward to working a 9 to 5 and soon discovered that it was really a 9 to 9 job.

I enjoyed getting to know the customers. I even met some fans that had followed my baseball career. I discovered that not only was I good at sales but my experiences in baseball made me a really good listener. Some of my customers asked if I could help their kids with pitching during my off hours. I was glad to help. The individualized pitching sessions were really fun. I became involved in several pitching clinics with many different youth groups.

The Unexpected

Although I was enjoying my job and working with kids during my off hours, my personal relationship had diminished. The highlight of my personal life was being able to spend a lot of quality time with my mother.   I especially enjoyed her home-cooked meals. My mother had recently celebrated her 55th birthday and unexpectedly had to be checked into the hospital after she complained about chest pains. We were all devastated to find out that she had to have her fourth bypass surgery. Around this same time I met Rochelle, a customer from the dealership. Her mother had gone through emergency bypass surgery six months earlier. Ironically, both of our mothers ended up at the same hospital, had the same surgeons and were in the same recovery areas, but they had never met. Rochelle and I would talk for hours and there was a sense of comfort in our conversations.

My mother had her first bypass surgery at the age of forty-three and over the years continued to have health problems. The doctors said that she only had one artery open and that the surgery was the only option. She had the surgery in late August of 1997 and came out of the surgery in stable condition. Unexpectedly, she took a turn for the worst and developed pneumonia. A trachea tube was inserted to assist her breathing. I went to visit her every day. My sisters and I would rotate visitation so she was never left alone. I remember going to see her and although she could not speak, I could tell that she knew I was there.
Late one evening, I received a phone call at home saying that I needed to return to the hospital because my mother's condition had deteriorated. When I arrived at the hospital, the doctors said

that her body was too weak to fight the pneumonia and that her body was shutting down. My mother passed away at the age of fifty-five on September 21, 1997.

Her funeral was held in the neighborhood where my mother had grown up at Wilson Park Christian Community Church. Pastor Sandy Blake Ushery did my mom's eulogy and knew our family well because we attended the church practically every Sunday as kids. I was amazed at how the processional into the church extended out of the front doors, down the sidewalk and down the street where my mother had once lived and I had played. My daughter and her mother flew in for the funeral. I believe that my mother was very proud of me not only because I was her son but because of the man that I had become. In fact, I'm sure she was proud of all of us.

I eventually broke up with my girlfriend and started focusing on creating a new chapter in my life. I was ready to start anew. My mother's death, the demise of my relationship with my girlfriend and my longing to move closer to my daughter who was living in Florida actually made baseball seem not as important as I thought it had been for so many years. I discovered that my dreams did not die when I left baseball. In fact, I was still a dreamer.

Turning Over A New Leaf

Rochelle and I started dating but we wanted things to move very slowly. We had both been married before and each of us had painful experiences in marriage. It didn't take long for me to realize that we were good for each other. Maybe our experiences made us more sensitive towards each other. However you look at it, our relationship was a pure blessing! Rochelle was able to add a level of calm to me as I was trying to maintain and improve my relationship with my daughter Taylor who had just turned 6. Rochelle had a son, Sterling, from her previous marriage. He was three years old.

Keeping the connection with Taylor was often made difficult while trying to negotiate visitation with my ex-wife. Ultimately, Taylor was allowed to visit twice a year and I never missed visiting her in January on her birthday. She came to Baltimore to visit for a few weeks in the summer and she also came for Christmas. I had to purchase three round trip tickets when Taylor came to visit. Rochelle would usually fly down to Florida to get Taylor then fly back with her to Baltimore. When it was time for Taylor to return home, I would usually fly with Taylor to Florida and return back home. When Taylor was at home in Florida, I kept in contact with her grandmother and her Aunt. They kept me informed of what was happening in her life. This communication put my mine at ease when she was not close to me.

On July 31, 2002, Rochelle and I were married in Jamaica. We decided on a private ceremony with just the two of us. I actually called and asked Taylor for her opinion. At the age of eleven, she was excited about the idea. Sterling was eight at the time and he was thrilled.

In September 2003, Rochelle and I discovered she was pregnant with twins. We couldn't wait to share the news with Taylor and Sterling. Unfortunately, we loss one of the babies, but we were re-assured that the other baby was still healthy. We waited until Taylor's visit that Christmas to share the news with her. We were quite surprised when Taylor was not quite as excited as we thought she would be. I reminded Taylor that no matter how many other children I had, she would never be replaced in my life. Pretty soon Taylor and Sterling were trying to pick out names and looking forward to the upcoming birth.

A few days before I visited Taylor for her birthday in January, my mother-in-law, Alma suffered a stroke while at home. Rochelle was on her way home from work when she received an urgent phone call from her sister. Their mother was being rushed to the hospital. Needless to say, it was a very stressful time. I was very concerned about Rochelle's physical and mental state since she was about 6 months pregnant at the time. I was told that my mother-in-law was in stable condition so I went to visit Taylor for her birthday. After I returned home from my visit with Taylor, my mother-in-law's condition worsened and she passed away on February 7, 2004.

My son, Daylin Alexander Smith was born late May, about 3 weeks before his due date by emergency c-section. It was Friday of the Memorial Day weekend and it was a very emotional day in more than one way. Although our newborn son had neither one his grandmother's alive to welcome him, we still felt the presence of both of our mother's love.

After the birth of my son, I was more determined than ever to complete a promise that I made to my mother many years ago. I promised her that I would write a book to describe my journey in baseball's Minor Leagues. At that time, I didn't realize that my experience in baseball was just the vehicle to my dream and that the real dream was to inspire others, especially young adults. I was fortunate to conduct a baseball clinic for youth from ages ten to sixteen for Winfield Baseball in Westminster, Maryland. During the baseball clinic I gave an inspirational talk to the group of young adults and their parents including a question and answer session that was well received. I continued to work with several youth groups including Northwood Baseball and Yankee Rebels Baseball both located in Baltimore, Maryland. After discussing my goals with my wife, we decided to create a company called Deeandro, LLC that would allow me to keep my promise to my mother to help women and youth programs through donations from motivational speaking engagements and youth advocacy. As a kick-off, we held our first annual Dreams Do Exist Golf Tournament at Oakmont Greens Golf Course in Hampstead, Maryland in July of 2008. The event included door prizes, raffle tickets, a chance to win a car, and a steak dinner. It was a huge success with many people coming together to support the cause of youth advocacy and to fellowship. As a result, Deeandro, LLC was able to make monetary donations to youth advocacy programs.

I am also a Certified Master and Senior Salesman for Lexus. I am also one of the top salesmen at Len Stoler Lexus of Owings Mills, Maryland. A Certified Master Salesman is required to have special training including tests to evaluate our knowledge of the Lexus brand, hands-on experience, great customer service skills and proven interpersonal skills. My work in sales has allowed me to stay in tune with a very diverse population.

The market today has drastically slowed down on domestic auto sales and to some degree on imported cars. The recession has affected the industry but I have a dedicated clientele base and I hope to stay in the industry. It is nice to know people and nice to be known. The economic impact on the car industry is unprecedented and my strong relationship with my clients has helped me maintain my client base.

In November of 2008, my wife and I stood in a line of hundreds of others for several hours to exercise our right to vote. I was impressed by Barack Obama's upbringing. It was similar to my own. I was once again reminded of how critical parental involvement is in the development of young people. We stayed up on election night watching the results and were elated by the historic results. Equally impressive was the concession speech from Senator John McCain, who acknowledged the momentous event. Senator McCain was hopeful that the many things that unite us as American was greater than the things that divide us!

Through my life experiences I have learned that adults play a pivotal role in forming a strong foundation for young people. Keeping dreams alive in our youths allows them to see beyond their present situation, which encourages them to live life to its fullest. It's also important that we teach the importance of giving back to others.

Dreams can become reality with support, dedication and motivation. The dreamer is still alive in me and I continue to pass on this message to all on a daily basis.

Daryl with the Padres Organization- 1985

Dreams Do Exist

Memorial Stadium - Mom & Me - 1983

Daryl at 9yrs in front of grandparents house

Daryl's Mom at Age 13

Daryl at 7 yrs old

Texas Rangers -1980 - Ist Season

Leave home for the first time -1980

Dreams Do Exist

1995- Game Day- Taiwan

Spring Training- Australia

Pitching Clinic with kids in Taiwan

1995- Taiwan -Live

1995- Taiwan -Live

Taiwan on the winning end!

Day off in Mexico

1981- Asheville

Instructional Baseball -Sarasota, Florida

Jr. Year at Northern High School -Baltimore, MD

1995- Spring Training

Singing National Athem- Memphis, TN

1995- Spring Training

Mom's Flight to Italy

My three sisters: Shell, Bay, Kareen

Championship Ring- 16 years & One Ring

1995- Spring Training

Dreams Do Exist

Kansas City Royals- Major League Debut -1990

 114 *Dreams Do Exist*

To Taylor!
From an admirer
XXOO
George S...

Dreams Do Exist

The Family: Taylor, Daryl, Daylin, Rochelle, Sterling

Cool, Calm & Collected

 115 *Dreams Do Exist*

Daryl Smith
Lifetime Dreamer

Dreams Do Exist

Daryl's Baseball Career Stats (United States only) – 1980 -1995*

*Statistics below does not include Winter ball, Off-season, or International play

Year	Team	Lg	Age	Org	Lvl	Unif	W	L	ERA	G	GS	CG	SH	GF	SV	IP	H	R	ER	HR	BB	SO	WP	H9	HR9	BB9	K9	WHIP
1980	RAN	GCL	19	Tex	Rk		1	1	4.5	4	2	0	0		0	12	13	9	6	0	4	4	2	9.8	0	3	3	1.42
	ASH	SAL	19	Tex	A		5	3	4.77	22	7	0	0		1	66	12	40	35	4	41	30	7	1.6	0.5	5.6	4.1	0.8
1981	ASH	SAL	20	Tex	A	-	16	5	2.76	29	22	7	0	4	1	160	136	65	49	7	57	64	9	7.7	0.4	3.2	3.6	1.21
1982	BUR	Midw	21	Tex	A		3	5	3.35	19	10	0	0	6	0	80.2	78	40	30	5	40	32	7	8.7	0.6	4.5	3.6	1.46
	TUL	Tex	21	Tex	AA		2	5	7.17	9	7	0	0	0	0	37.2	51	35	30	4	24	18	5	12	1	5.7	4.3	1.99
1983	SAL	Caro	22	Sd	A+		1	2	4.2	13	3	1	1	2	1	55.2	53	30	26	3	32	35	5	8.6	0.5	5.2	5.7	1.53
	TUL	Tex	22	Tex	AA		0	0	1.88	6	1	0	0	2	0	14.1	14	3	3	1	6	5	0	8.8	0.6	3.8	3.1	1.4
1984	SAL	Caro	23	Tex	A+		6	3	4.3	16	12	0	0	1	0	67	67	40	32	6	44	38	10	9	0.8	5.9	5.1	1.66
	TUL	Tex	23	Tex	AA	-	0	1	14.4	7	0	0	0	1	0	10.2	18	17	17	0	9	6	3	15	0	7.6	5.1	2.53
1985	WAT	Midw	24	Cle	A		0	0	1.93	1	0	0	0	0	0	4.2	4	1	1	1	2	5	0	7.7	1.9	3.9	9.7	1.29
	WAT	East	24	Cle	AA		2	2	3.52	16	6	1	0	8	4	53.2	42	25	21	5	37	38	5	7	0.8	6.2	6.4	1.47
1986	WAT	East	25	Cle	AA		4	3	3.54	21	11	4	1	4	0	89	71	37	35	8	48	55	11	7.2	0.8	4.9	5.6	1.34
1987	WLL & REA	East	26	Cle/Phi	AA		7	3	3.92	21	14	1	0	2	1	87.1	86	46	38	6	46	58	6	8.9	0.6	4.7	6	1.51
	MAI	IL	26	Phi	AAA	-	1	3	6.75	4	4	0	0	0	0	22.2	21	18	17	4	13	16	0	8.3	1.6	5.2	6.4	1.5
1988	BIR	Sou	27	Chw	AA		1	4	3.23	40	0	0	0	33	7	53	42	25	19	0	27	44	6	7.1	0	4.6	7.5	1.3
1990	MEM	Sou	29	Kc	AA		2	1	3.17	21	0	0	0	5	1	48.1	46	27	17	1	23	48	10	8.6	0.2	4.3	8.9	1.43
	OMA	Amer	29	Kc	AAA		6	2	3.09	11	10	0	0	0	0	64	59	25	22	4	32	56	3	8.3	0.6	4.5	7.9	1.42
	KC	AL	29	Kc	MLB	40	0	1	4.05	2	1	0	0	1	0	6.2	5	3	3	0	4	6	0	6.8	0	5.4	8.1	1.35
1991	OMA	Amer	30	Kc	AAA		4	5	3.39	23	14	0	0	4	0	93	82	38	35	10	33	94	4	7.9	1	3.2	9.1	1.24
1993	BOW	East	32	Bal	AA		0	0	2.45	3	3	0	0	0	0	22	14	7	6	1	11	23	0	5.7	0.4	4.5	9.4	1.14
1995	COL	IL	34	Nyy	AAA	-	0	3	4.03	13	7	0	0	2	0	51.1	54	31	23	5	20	23	5	9.5	0.9	3.5	4	1.44

Daryl's Baseball Career Stats (United States only) – 1980 -1995*

*Statistics below does not include Winter ball, Off-season, or International play

	W	L	ERA	G	GS	CG	SH	GF	SV	IP	H	R	ER	HR	BB	SO	WP	H9	HR9	BB9	K9	WHIP
Major League Totals - 1 Season(s)	0	1	4.05	2	1	0	0	1	0	6.2	5	3	3	0	4	6	0	6.7	0	5.4	8.1	1.35
Minor League Totals - 13 Season(s)	61	51	3.8	299	133	14	2		16	1093	963	559	462	75	549	692	98	7.9	0.6	4.5	5.7	1.38

Rookie

Gulf Coast Rangers - 1

A

Asheville Tourists - 2 (Career Leader - 21 Wins as of 04/20/09)
Burlington Rangers - 1

A+

Salem Redbirds - 2

AA

Birmingham Barons - 1
Bowie Baysox - 1
Memphis Chicks - 1

AAA

Columbus Clippers - 1
Maine Guides - 1
Omaha Royals - 2

Major League
Kansas City Royals - 1

Daryl C. Smith
Deeandro, Inc.

Born July 29, 1960, in the city of Baltimore, Maryland, Daryl Clinton Smith had a far from ordinary life. From his 16 year career as a professional baseball player to his current role as a Certified Master Sales Associate for Lexus, Daryl has made time for his loving wife Rochelle, three wonderful children, and much more. Daryl is a community man enriching lives through youth advocacy.

Throughout his life, Daryl has been active in such organizations as Big Brothers of Baltimore, Broward Juvenile Detention Center in Florida, and Youth Services International in Parkville, Maryland. His lifetime goals continue to include helping kids find their niche, and enriching lives through mentorship and youth athletic programs.

Daryl lists his daughter Taylor's acceptance to Monmouth University on a full academic and basketball scholarship, his son Sterling's acceptance to Western Technical School of Environmental Sciences, and his youngest son Daylin's entering pre-school as his proudest accomplishments. They are all growing up to be dreamers just like their dad!

In his spare time, Daryl has written his biography entitled, "Dreams Do Exist", an inspirational journey for all of us. This book is a personal recount of the daily trials he encountered during his time as a minor and major league baseball player. "Dreams Do Exist" is filled with real life lessons that are relevant to both youths and adults.

www.dreamsdoexist.com

Corporate Sponsors

Ace Uniform Services, Inc *Buddy Finkelstein* *Baltimore, MD 21230* *1 (800) 366 1616*	*Audio Connection* *1735 E. Joppa Road* *Towson, MD 21234* *(410) 661-1580*	*Autolines* *Custom Auto Pin Striping* *Derrick Restivo* *(410) 598 1234*
Beltway Leather & Vinyl *Repair* *Dave Mansfield* *(410) 521-1758*	*Best Western - Security* *1800 Belmont Avenue* *Baltimore, MD USA 21244* *(410)-265-1400*	*Bingoworld* *Randy Clemens* *4901 Bellegrove Road* *Glen Burnie, MD 21221* *(410) 636 0290*
Blue Point Crab House *11412 Reisterstown Road* *Owings Mills, MD* *(410) 363-8444*	*Brittany & Crystal Beauty* *Salon* *4910 Liberty Heights Avenue* *Baltimore, Maryland 21207* *(410) 664-4413*	*Complete Clutter Care* *1 Windblown Court* *Baltimore, Maryland 21209* *(443) 414-4124*
D & E Custom Framing *1907 Woodlawn Drive* *Baltimore, MD 21207* *(410) 298 6262*	*DBA Cash Plus* *7603 Harford Road* *Baltimore, MD 21234* *(410) 319 7700*	*Extr-A-Care* *Pharmacy & Medical* *Equipment* *801 Park Avenue* *Baltimore, MD 21201* *(410) 332 4666*
The Five Mile House *5302 Reisterstown Road* *Baltimore, MD 21215* *(410) 578-0075*	*Flemings Steakhouse* *720 Aliceanna St.* *Baltimore MD 21202* *(410) 332-1666*	*Floyd's 99 Barbers* *9050 Baltimore National Pike* *Suite 102* *Ellicott City, MD 21042* *(410) 313-8420*
The Glass Man *Marcus Levinson* *(888) 819 5111*	*Golf Galaxy – Towson* *803 Goucher Blvd* *Towson, MD 21286* *(443) 279 3733*	*Great Moments, Inc* *140 Village Shopping Center* *531-B Jermor Lane* *Westminister, MD 21157* *(410) 876-6906*
Larry Stevens World of Art *Harborplace* *301 Light Street* *Baltimore, MD 21202* *(410) 780-5474*	*Melba's Place* *3126 Greenmount Avenue* *Baltimore, MD 21218* *(410) 366-6536*	*Optical Center* *1100 Reisterstown Road* *Pikesville, MD 21208* *(410) 484-8700*
Play It Again Sports *9150-3 Baltimore National* *Pike* *Ellicott City, MD 21042* *(410) 418-9371*	*Robbie's First Base* *9 West Ridgely Road* *Lutherville, MD 21093* *(410) 560 3200*	*SportClips* *10357 Reisterstown Road* *between Owings Mills Blvd &* *Rosewood Lane* *(410) 857-4339*
Sugar Plum Confections *Contact: Konya I.* *Lindsey(301) 659 9119* *www.sugarplum-* *confections.com*	*Tom's Sports Tavern* *9307 Liberty Road* *Randallstown, MD* *(410) 922-4489*	*Westminister Cigar Shop* *23 E. Main Street* *Westminister, MD 21157* *(410) 876 4786* *11700-B Reisterstown Road* *Owings Mills, MD 21117* *(410) 517 0555*

Dreams Do Exist

Tatyana Goldberg
1852 Reisterstown Road, # 202
Pikesville, MD
(410) 653 - 1700

Dreams Do Exist

Play It Again Sports

9150-3 Baltimore National Pike

Ellicott City, MD   21042

(410) 418 - 9371

Accurate Glass Tinting

11500 Reisterstown Road

Owings Mills, MD   21117

(410) 922 - 1889